Faith: Security and Risk

*The Dynamics
of
Spiritual Growth*

by

Richard W. Kropf

Paulist Press
New York 🕊 *Mahwah*

Library of Congress Cataloging-in-Publication Data

Kropf, Richard W., 1932–
    Faith: security and risk : the dynamics of spiritual growth/by Richard W. Kropf.
      p. cm.
    Includes bibliographical references and index.
    ISBN 0-8091-3178-1
    1. Faith—Psychology. 2. Faith—Psychology—History of doctrines—20th century. 3. Christianity—Psychology. I. Title.
BT772.K69 1990
248′.01—dc20   90-34989
                                                 CIP

Published by Paulist Press
997 Macarthur Boulevard
Mahwah, New Jersey 07430

Printed and bound in the
United States of America

Contents

Contents

Acknowledgements

I would like to express my thanks to those friends who have encouraged me, especially Sr. Donna Kushtush, O.P., who first introduced me to the work of James Fowler some years before the publication of his first major book, and to those who read through much of this book in its initial and later stages of development, especially Bruce Gotts, Tim Uhlman, Tony Morse, and Shelly FitzGerald. I also owe a debt to Fr. Larry Boadt at Paulist Press, under whose advice and guidance the manuscript finally reached publication, and many thanks to Mary Flinn for her final checking of the manuscript and the taxing task of reading the proofs.

All scriptural quotations, unless otherwise noted, are from *The Jerusalem Bible,* edited by Alexander Jones or *The New Jerusalem Bible,* edited by Henry Wansbrough, both published by Doubleday and Company, 1966 and 1985.

Passages from *The Teachings of the Second Vatican Council* are as edited by Gregory Baum, and published by The Newman Press in 1963.

I also wish to acknowledge the following publishers and holders of copyrights:

The Bollingen Foundation for material taken from *The Collected Works of C.G. Jung,* published in the United States by Princeton University Press;

Crossroad Press for material from Avery Dulles, *The Survival of Dogma,* 1982;

Doubleday and Company for material from Hans Küng's *Theology for the Third Millennium: An Ecumenical View,* translated by Peter Heinegg (1988);

Harper and Row for James W. Fowler's *Stages of Faith: The Psychology of Human Development and the Quest for Meaning* (1981) and *Becoming Adult, Becoming Christian: Adult Development and Christian Faith* (1984); and for the passage quoted from Paul Tillich's *The Dynamics of Faith* (1957);

Herder and Herder for passages from Pierre Babin's *The Crisis of Faith: The Religious Psychology of Adolescence,* translation by Eva Fleischner, 1963;

The Institute for Carmelite Studies for a quotation from *The Collected Works of St. John of the Cross* translated by Kieran Kavanaugh and Otilio Rodriguez (1973);

New American Library for material taken from Viktor E. Frankl's *The Will to Meaning: Foundations and Applications of Logotherapy* (1969);

W.W. Norton for selections from Erik Erikson's *Young Man Luther* (1958) and *Gandhi's Truth* (1969);

Random House/Vintage publishers for the quotations from: Alan Watts, *The Wisdom of Insecurity,* originally published by Pantheon Books, 1951; Viktor Frankl, *The Doctor and the Soul: From Psychotherapy to Logotherapy,* originally published by Alfred A. Knopf, Inc., (1955, 1965).

The Religious Education Association of the United States and Canada for information taken from the 1985 study *Faith Development in the Adult Life Cycle* produced in conjunction with the Gallup Organization;

Simon and Schuster, for passages taken from Viktor E. Frankl's *The Unconscious God: Psychotherapy and Theology* (1975);

Viking Penguin Co. for the passage quoted from the 1970 edition of Abraham Maslow's *Religions, Values, and Peak Experiences* (from *The Further Reaches of Human Nature,* copyright 1971 by Bertha G. Maslow).

Introduction

There is a story in three of the four gospels about Jesus coming to the apostles by walking across the Sea of Galilee. But only the gospel of St. Matthew (8:21–28) relates how Peter challenged Jesus to identify himself by bidding Peter to meet him by walking on the water as well. Having climbed over the side of the boat and ventured out to meet Jesus, Peter had second thoughts about what he was doing, began to sink beneath the waves, panicked and cried out for Jesus to save him. Then Jesus, after rescuing him, upbraided him for being a "man of little faith."

This story raises some very probing questions about faith. Was Peter really engaged in an act of faith or foolhardiness? What was the impetuous apostle really thinking of? Was it really the Lord who was approaching them across those stormy waves or was it an apparition of some kind or even the figment of their own frightened imaginations? Peter had to know for sure, for himself. There could be no passive waiting for him. Yet, almost immediately, aghast at the risk to his own life and paralyzed by fright, Peter began to sink. Seeking the assurance of the Lord's presence, Peter had risked himself, only to flounder in the waves of doubt. Was it really Peter's *faith* or was it a *lack* of faith that had impelled him to want to walk across the water to meet this strange figure that approached them? Why couldn't he be content like the others to wait and see? Was not the temporary security of the storm-tossed boat enough? Why insist on the additional insurance of the Lord's presence when months before, on that same lake, Jesus had insisted that *faith* itself was all that was needed?

How like Peter we all are, even if we lack his boldness. Often we seem to believe, only to doubt and lose courage when the going gets rough. There is an inborn tendency in us to seek the *security* that faith would provide and, at the same time, a profound aversion to take the risks involved. If Peter's brash act of faith failed to meet the test, perhaps it was because Jesus required of him a greater test of trust—or of patience. But one thing is sure: whatever was required of him involved a risk and at the same time a commitment. Once venturing out on his chosen path of faith, Peter could not afford to turn back or to lose courage, except at yet a greater risk. Faith, and life, are like that.

So we can not avoid risk. The American philosopher and psychologist William James saw this only too clearly. James' idea of faith, as we shall see, was based on the pragmatic idea of "nothing risked, nothing gained." We cannot advance spiritually (or any other way in this life) unless we are willing to let go of the *security* that so often binds us to what is familiar and comfortable. In other words, faith involves risk. Faith, then—at least a living faith—is not so much a thing as an attitude or a way of life. And like life itself, it is always on the move, always reaching out toward the future. "To live is to change," said Cardinal Newman, "and to have lived fully is to have changed often." Whatever doesn't change is already dead. Faith is alive only when it grows, develops, and continually matures.

If I have briefly turned to William James as someone who both underscored the dynamic idea of faith and underlined its dangers, I have turned to Viktor Frankl even more to show how this dynamic works in our life and on every level of faith. Ever since I first read Frankl's own engaging account of his survival of the Nazi concentration camps many years back, I have been convinced that his personal story, as well as his theories, contains the essence of what the life of faith is all about. Over the years I have attempted to apply his insights to several aspects of the spiritual life, but it is only now that I have attempted to apply his thought, along with some ideas borrowed from theologians Paul Tillich and Avery Dulles, to a more thorough understanding of the structure and dynamics of faith. Yet, if this book of mine were to be dedicated to anyone, I think Viktor Frankl would be the most deserving of credit.

As far as the stages of faith development used in this present book, they are based for the most part on the work of James Fowler and his colleagues, as well as inspired by the pioneering work done by forerunners in developmental psychology such as Erik Erikson, Jean Piaget, and Lawrence Kohlberg, along with others who have been brainstorming in this field as of late. I should stress that my contribution is not meant either to endorse the work of all these researchers as being the last word on this topic or, on the other hand, to try to critique their findings in any serious way—I am hardly in a position to do so. Much the same could be said of the earlier work of Pierre Babin in France upon which I have drawn. I only use their work as a handy framework or scheme with which I can elaborate some of the major variations and implications of Frankl's central insight as it applies to the life of faith and spiritual growth.

So what this book most of all proposes to do is not so much to spell out all the details of the various stages or levels of faith as to try to help the reader understand *why* it is that all too often our faith fails to develop as it should. In this respect faith development becomes synonymous with "spiritual development" or growth in spirituality, even holiness. In this vein, even my use of Frankl, like my use of the latest in developmental research and theory, is primarily meant to help us understand the particular challenges that face us at each stage in hopes that we will be able to guide ourselves to a more mature spiritual life as well as a better understanding of the psychodynamics of faith.

It is here, especially when it comes to the higher reaches of spirituality, that we come full circle and will find, I maintain, that the wisdom of the great mystics and religious thinkers of the past remains eternally valid even while understood in a new light. Thus what I have borrowed from

Frankl is only a new restatement of the central truth behind *all* religious faith, when it is actually and authentically lived. And I say this of all faiths and all religions, although as a Christian I naturally put it in gospel terms first.

> Unless a grain of wheat falls into the earth and dies,
> it remains only a single grain. But if it dies, it yields
> a rich harvest (Jn 12:24).

This same truth has been stated in many ways, not only in the gospels but in the sacred writings of the major religions throughout the world. I believe that the life, death, and resurrection of Jesus was this same "word" made incarnate, this same divine and human message in concrete form. It only remains for us to put it into practice in our own lives.

1. Faith and Happiness

> Success and *happiness* must *happen,* and the less
> one cares for them, the more they can.
>
> Viktor Frankl, *The Will to Meaning*

Everyone seeks happiness. So fundamental is this fact
of existence that America's founding fathers not only accepted this classical principle as "self-evident," but even
held "the pursuit of happiness" to be a basic human right.
The idea that humans by nature seek happiness is at least as
ancient as the philosopher Socrates who insisted that no one
acts in any fashion unless he or she believes, rightly or
wrongly, that what one does will bring happiness.

Often, of course, people have mistaken notions about
what is good for them or will make them happy. Mere physical pleasure is often wrongly equated with happiness. But, as
Aristotle pointed out, pleasure really is nothing but an indicator of what should be, but is not always, a source of happiness for us. As we soon discover, immediate pleasure can
very often end up being a false indicator, or even a trap that
destroys the really valuable things in life. Just as the attractions of certain foods and beverages, for example, can end
up causing us to destroy the health that food and drink are
meant to preserve, so too we also know that many really
worthwhile goals in life can be reached only through the
pain of great effort or through the cost of long periods of
sometimes boring preparation.

So when we speak about human happiness we are not
talking about the immediate gratification of our cravings for
pleasure, or even about avoidance of unnecessary pain.
Many of our pains are, to be sure, unnecessary. But many of
our postponed pleasures (and for the immature, such post-
ponement is often only seen as pain) as well as our hardships

5

are for the sake of a much greater and more lasting happiness—something that we nowadays are apt to call "fulfillment."

But the meaning of "fulfillment" is not self-evident either. For some, fulfillment means cramming in all the pleasures and experiences one possibly can into a lifetime—and as quickly as possible, just in case one doesn't live very long. For others, fulfillment seems to take the shape of living as long as possible, even if one deprives oneself of the possibility of accomplishing anything else in life.

Still, as we are all too well aware, life is limited. As the psalmist reminds us "our years are seventy, or if we are strong, eighty" (Ps 90). Today, now that this biblical lifespan has almost become a fact, not just for the lucky few who once made it to adulthood but for whole populations of modern industrialized nations, people have become more and more concerned not just about mere survival on the one hand, or immediate pleasure on the other. Today more and more people think of their long-term happiness. Such happiness is seen increasingly as the fulfillment of our own individual potentialities, or in becoming precisely that unique person that God and nature have destined us to be. As a result, the search for fulfillment has become a major industry of the modern world.

Now you may ask: What does all this have to do with faith? Quite a lot, actually—and in more than just one way.

For one, *faith,* in the broad sense of believing that something is possible, has everything to do with it. We would hardly even begin to seek happiness or fulfillment if we didn't think it is possible to find it. In a way, it is something like starting up a business, or even like betting on the lottery—unless you believe success is possible, you will not even bother to try. And without some trying (despite books titled ". . . without even trying") it is very unlikely you'll succeed.

For another, when it comes to seeking long-term happiness or fulfillment, faith, in the religious sense of the word, has always had everything to do with people's hopes of a happiness or fulfillment that somehow escapes death. Generally, such hope has been expressed in terms of faith in there being some kind of heaven, be it in terms of a happy-hunting ground, a Valhalla of the heroes, a paradise of the saved, "the bosom of Abraham," or even the state of "nirvana." And while some religions have been rather vague about what happens after death, most religions have had a great deal to say as to how to cope with death—even if by trying to ignore it.

Yet here we run into a great paradox or contradiction. Most of the great or "higher" religions, when it comes to facing this bottom line, are unanimous in preaching one conclusion: that however you think of an afterlife—if you think of one at all—the true key to achieving happiness or fulfillment is to be found in *self-transcendence,* or the forgetting of self.

This is not an easy truth to accept. It comes down to saying that if you want to be happy, then you must forget about being happy. If you are seeking fulfillment, then the quickest way to achieve it is to forget about it. Of course, we cannot just come out and say that and expect to be believed. And if people took this paradox at face value, the whole self-improvement industry would collapse overnight. And, no doubt, most of the churches would lose a lot of their followers as well.

Nevertheless, when all is said and done, we will find that this paradox is the core truth of all genuine religion, that "he who would save his life will lose it; but he who loses his life ... shall save it" (Lk 9:24). I could cite many similar passages from the Bible, from the other sacred scriptures of the world, the writings of mystics and saints, and even of the philosophers, all of which come down to saying the same thing.

The problem is that so many if not all of these sayings

seem to come from another time, another place—from another world from that of modern persons. Despite what Socrates, Buddha, or even Jesus and the great saints had to say,
we are still apt to write them off all the more because they
appear to be exceptional, almost as if they were not men and
women like ourselves, struggling to find their own happiness or fulfillment in life.

Part of our problem is that although we are perhaps
willing to admit the ultimate truth of this paradox, we are
not really sure *why* this is true. Nor are we really convinced
that it has any practical application in our ordinary lives, so
we are all too apt to fail to see how it most of all applies in the
life of faith. To try to remedy this situation, I turn first of all
to the life-work and teaching of the internationally known
and acclaimed psychiatrist, Viktor E. Frankl.

Faith and the Search for Meaning

As a Jew, born and raised in Vienna, a survivor of the
Nazi death camps, Frankl suffered personally through a life
crisis which not only confirms our thesis but throws great
light on what it means to be a person of faith.

Frankl's insight is as simple as it is devastating. It is
basically that human happiness or fulfillment cannot be
successfully pursued; it can only "ensue"—which is to say
that it can only come to us as a *by-product* of *meaning*.

By "meaning," Frankl meant whatever *reason* or *purpose* that each of us has for living. But this reason or purpose
must be present *in our minds*. For while we may vaguely
believe or somehow take it for granted that there is an overall purpose for the scheme of things in this universe, unless
this purpose translates itself into a conscious meaning for
my own life, right here and now, that overall purpose does
me no good—it cannot make me feel happy or fulfilled unless I know about it and deliberately relate myself to it.

But how are we to come to a knowledge of such a purpose or higher meaning in our lives? For those who give thought to such matters, this purpose or meaning presents itself as a *problem,* but to an even greater extent it remains a *mystery.* Problems can be, to some extent solved, but mysteries have to be *lived.* The purpose of life, for each of us, can be such a problem, but the overall meaning of life, as well as our place in it, remains such a mystery. And as such, it reveals itself through life itself, and this experience turns out to be the experience of faith.

Too often we find this same lesson, again and again, suppressed, forgotten, or otherwise consigned into oblivion in the midst of the distractions of ordinary life and the ritualizing of beliefs. Like us, Frankl suspected this truth and even planned to write a major book on the subject. But as it turned out, he first had to live out this truth in its fullest dimension in the midst of the excruciating trials of the concentration camp. His lived experience of this ancient mystery can be a new revelation of this truth for us all.

Perhaps many are already familiar with his story as told in his autobiographical sketch and introduction to his thought, *Man's Search for Meaning.* Yet the directly religious implications of this extraordinary story are often overlooked. Readers easily grasp his primary point: only *meaning* gives purpose to life, and to be happy, one must seek that meaning in something, some cause, or some purpose greater than one's own selfish desire to be happy. What they so often fail to see, however, is that in the end only one purpose or only one center of meaning proves capable of fulfilling this need in any permanent way.

We need only recall the succession of purposes or meanings for which Frankl was determined to survive in order to quickly grasp this point. At first he naively thought he would have much time in prison for writing, so he sewed his manuscript for his book into the lining of his overcoat, only to have it confiscated almost immediately. Next, he resolved to survive to be reunited with his wife, only to soon realize that she, also a prisoner, was not robust enough to survive. Soon after, he dedicated himself to helping keep prisoners alive; if you could work, the SS wouldn't execute you outright—at least not till the end. But then, as the Nazis began to panic at the advance of the Allied forces, they began to compound their horrendous crime by executing, right and left, every prisoner that they thought they could dispose of. At this point, a series of circumstances offered the opportunity for what Frankl hoped might turn out to be at least a slim chance of escape. But instead he hesitated, electing to stay with his fellow prisoners. It turned out that those who accepted the offer to be trucked away to a "rest camp" to await liberation were really being taken out for their execution. Frankl survived when his camp was overrun by the liberating forces before the SS could dispose of the rest of them. Ironically, Frankl lived because he was willing to die with the rest.

Why did Frankl decide to stay? Of course, he suspected a ruse in the offer to leave. But at least it offered a possible avenue of escape, whereas to stay in the camp seemed to offer only certain death. Frankl said that he estimated his chances of survival at that point as less than one in twenty. Yet, stay he did. Why? Frankl put it in these terms: he had already reached a point where he began to see a meaning in what was the apparent certainty of his own death. When he had accepted the offer to work in the prison camp hospital, despite others warning him that this might only hasten his death, he decided that it was better to die in the effort to keep others alive than to die simply as a victim of a passively accepted fate.

Although Frankl did not claim to have been a particularly religious man at this point in his life, his story reveals him as a man of deep faith and that he was even able to convey this faith to others. In reading his account of these last days of his ordeal, it is almost as if he was subconsciously drawing on the biblical tradition of the mysterious "suffering servant" in the later chapters of the book of Isaiah, whose ordeal and death proves redemptive not only for his own people, but also for the whole world (see Is 52:13–53:12). And although Frankl preferred not to advertise what his own beliefs might be, it is evident from his own story as well as in his later writings, that religion—or, more exactly, *faith* centered around religious hopes—provides the final and ultimately unassailable guarantee of meaning.

How essential to human life, then, is faith in some transcendental purpose? Frankl relates how some of his fellow prisoners managed to survive by living for less ultimate, even though worthy, goals. One, for example, lived to be reunited with his family, but only to return to his town to be told that they had all perished in the war; he killed himself. Others survived for other reasons, some of them undoubtedly lesser ones. But the point is that only a reason or a meaning that will survive all eventualities, even one's own death, is fully adequate. The other purposes, no matter how effective they may be under limited conditions, are not enough in the face of death.

But is it necessary to believe explicitly in "life everlasting" to face death with composure? Perhaps not. For some, it is enough to have "lived well," whatever that may mean. But whatever that great beyond may be—joy, fulfillment or even punishment, or simply nothingness or oblivion— somehow our purpose or reason for existence has to measure up to the demand for meaning. That this meaning remains somewhat ambiguous or enshrouded in mystery is what touches on the essence of faith. For the minute that I set out to know, beyond all doubt, the happiness or security of being *absolutely sure, for myself,* of this meaning or purpose of my life, it is most apt to escape me.

Thus, again, the paradox, but in another way—the knowledge or consciousness of this meaning or purpose cannot be generally proved or demonstrated logically beyond all doubt. Indeed, in his new preface to his earliest book, Frankl defines *religion* as "man's search for *ultimate* meaning" and "belief and faith as *trust* in ultimate meaning." There can be no question, then, that for Frankl the search for happiness or meaning is ultimately the quest of faith (*The Unconscious God: Psychotherapy and Theology,* p. 13). To live without meaning, as Frankl contends in his many books, is to court the danger of being in the grip of an "existential neurosis," to exist under a pervasive cloud of purposelessness that reveals itself in frenzied activity, superficial living, inane pursuits, and, not infrequently, phobias of one sort or another.

Yet we must ask ourselves what kind of meaning suffices. Must it always be an "ultimate meaning"? No doubt, as Frankl admitted, under the normal conditions of life, purposes or goals that in some way supply a meaning are often found in forms that fall far short of religious convictions or profound philosophies of life. Many, if not almost all, people invest meaning in having raised a family or in having a circle of friends. Many others concentrate on their business or profession. Some simply claim nothing more but to live for the sake of living, while others deepen the richness of life through love of nature, music, literature, or other cultural expressions. But on the other hand, some even seem to find their life's meaning in merely collecting things, be it old magazines, postage stamps, rocks, beer cans, matchbooks, or just plain junk. So the test of meaning is whether such purposes or goals truly contribute to the quality or depth of life. While the best of them may seem like worthy goals, too often some of these become mere diversions that prevent us from really having lived. We may get our names in *The Guinness Book of Records* and even take a certain satisfaction in that. But to the degree that these goals or purposes fail to pass the test of *ultimacy* they are bound to disappoint. Yet the prevalence of these "existential neuroses," particularly in affluent societies, indicates that there is a crisis of meaning in modern life. The question arises: How has this come about?

The Quest for Self-Fulfillment

Frankl's ideas, with their appeal to lived experience, definitely imply a particular philosophical view of human existence. Much of modern thought on the subject of happiness is a popularization of the thought of two of Frankl's forerunners in Vienna, Sigmund Freud and Alfred Adler. If Freud and Adler eventually agreed to disagree, hence founding two differing schools of psychiatry, then we can say that Frankl's approach differed in a way that is unique in modern philosophy. We should make no bones about it: these differing approaches to psychiatry and psychology are in the end, radically different philosophies of life.

The weakness in Freud's system, according to Frankl, is that it is focused primarily on the "pleasure principle" as the central motive of human conduct. In this line of thinking, human happiness consists in a balance between felt needs and their fulfillment as measured in terms of pleasurable satisfaction in our lives. For Freud the *will-to-pleasure* constitutes the primary life-force, and the satisfaction of our pleasure needs, symbolized primarily in sexual terms, is the major motivation of life.

Adler, on the other hand, focused not so much on pleasurable motivations and results as on the development of the human potential understood as a drive for self-determination. Instead of pleasurable satisfaction of biological needs, for Adler the expression of human *will* or the *will-to-power* is much more important. Adler's views, much more than Freud's, have led to the present-day concentration on the subject of *"self-actualization"* and the great profusion of books and techniques promising "self-fulfillment."

In Frankl's estimation, neither Freud nor Adler is entirely wrong. But people who gear their lives to the pursuit of pleasure make a big mistake, according to Frankl, not just because they've really fallen into a hedonistic, and often selfish, form of life, but even more, if one chooses to remain selfish, it just doesn't work—or if it seems to at first, it doesn't last for long. Such concern for our own pleasure or satisfaction, instead of fulfilling us, ends by driving us back on our own limitations, like a child who gets sick on too much ice cream or sweets, or an adult who pursues his or her own satisfactions to the point that they no longer entertain but become boring instead. The Freudian dynamic is flawed by underrating the deeper potentialities of human existence.

Does Adler's approach do any better? To some extent, in Frankl's estimation, it is more on the right track. It is not so much happiness or fulfillment that can be measured in pleasure that people really crave, but much more the satisfaction of living their own lives to the fullest, even when this may involve quite a lot of pain. This fulfillment of the human urge to exist, to be, and to have their existence make a difference is a much more serious business than any pursuit of pleasure. As the Adlerian school sees it, there can be no lasting satisfaction or pleasure at the expense of denying one's "real self," the self that one is capable of being.

The problem with the Alderian school of thought is, however, that as necessary a goal as self-actualization may be, it is still concerned primarily with *one's own self.* Even in the midst of what may seem to be heroic self-denial of the lesser pleasures in life—and sometimes of the greater ones as well—it is still, at the root, a selfish or egocentric approach. It is still primarily a quest for self-satisfaction or self-fulfillment, however disguised in a search for a more worthy and more lasting goal.

So in the end, Adler's approach only differs from the Freudian view in one important way and that is in the emphasis that it places on what is more directly the *means* or instrument used (the executive self) for finding fulfillment instead of the satisfaction or other pleasurable pay-offs that generally accompany it. Put in terms of corporate success, Adler's approach would have us concentrate on the power and prestige, instead of the size of the salary or other "perks" that go along with the position. Thus both the Freudian and the Adlerian approaches are not only tailor-made for the "me generation," they may have been, to a large degree, responsible for it.

To illustrate how Frankl's view, with its insistence on self-transcendence, diametrically opposes those of Freud and Adler when it comes to this basic issue, I will borrow from some illustrations in another book of Frankl's, *The Will to Meaning*. In his diagrams, which I have combined and added to, we have the basic directions of his thought:

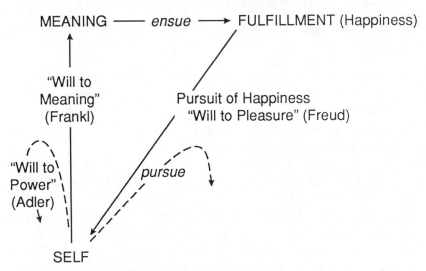

At the lower left-hand of the illustration, I have added the "self" as a help toward understanding where we our-selves fit into the picture. Notice that the solid line arrows give the basic direction of Frankl's thought, while the broken line arrows indicate the faulty paths. The pursuit of happiness, understood particularly in terms of Freud's pleasure-principle, fails to lead to any lasting fulfillment. The arrow of Adler's "Will-to-Power" starts off in the right direction but falls back on the self—particularly in the more recent interpretations of this term.

As I have indicated by the direction of the arrows in the diagram, the flow of energy must be consistently *clockwise*. If we make the mistake of trying to move around the diagram counter-clockwise we shall not only miss the central point of our whole discussion of Frankl and his thought, but we shall find ourselves also misunderstanding and, what is worse, misleading ourselves on what we imagine is the path of faith.

Meaning and Transcendence

In his introduction to one of his earlier books, Frankl wrote:

> Man lives in three dimensions: the somatic, the mental, and the spiritual. The spiritual dimension cannot be ignored, for it is what makes us human (*The Doctor and the Soul: From Psychotherapy to Logotherapy*).

As we shall see, there is really nothing new in this statement. True meaning or purpose, if it is to be worthy of our capacity for full human existence, has to be found in a form that surpasses whatever level of existence that we now enjoy or suffer. Frankl used the word *logos* (the ancient Greek term for the guiding *reason* or *intelligence* that directs the universe) for this meaning or purpose in life. It is this something that is greater than ourselves which alone can fully call forth our capacity to become fully what we are capable of.

If Freud's approach to happiness or self-fulfillment is flawed, it is not just because it is defective psychologically speaking; it is even more lacking as a philosophy of life. It simply underestimates human capacity and needs. At its root the Freudian philosophy of life is primarily concerned with what the ancient philosophers called the *somatic* or bodily level of existence, reducing the meaning of human existence to the satisfaction of needs which, although they have their psychological aspects, are, at root, physical in nature.

Adler's approach is, as we said, more on target, being concerned with the human need to be a self-determined person in one's own right. Adler's "will-to-power," translated as "self-actualization" by his American disciple, Carl R. Rogers (see *On Becoming a Person*), points to the human need to *become* more rather than simply to have or enjoy more. But it too falls short. It focuses on what is more properly psychological or the "mental" dimension in human nature, but is this enough? For Frankl, obviously not.

Here Frankl, again adapting the language of the ancient philosophers, saw something more to human nature than simply the body (*soma*) and soul or mind (*psyche* or *nous*). We also possess the *pneuma* or "spirit." And it is this spiritual dimension that alone makes us fully human.

But here we must interject a crucial theological point. Basing himself on the ancient Hebrew concept that it is God's spirit or breath (the *Ruah Yahweh*) that alone brings things to life, St. Paul tells us that it is our *pneuma,* the human "spirit," that reaches out to God's *Pneuma,* the Holy Spirit, and which alone can bring us to our full destiny as "children of God" (see Rom 8:16). In other words, the three levels or dimensions of human existence are not by any means complete. On the spiritual level, in particular, we are not whole or complete persons. Our "spirit" by itself exists more as a capacity or potentiality than as an actuality or finished product.

Or if we were to rephrase St. Paul in modern scientific terms, we might say that while the evolution of life has brought us beyond the merely biological stage of existence to the psychological level, we remain unsatisfied and we, whether as individuals or as a species, not only are still in the process of trying to become merely more human, but even, to some extent, depending on how you look at it, super-human. In any case, we are trying to evolve beyond what we presently are. Culture, religion, science, technology, and even the current craze for self-fulfillment all point in this direction.

The implications of this point of view are tremendous. Whether viewed in theological, philosophical, or even simply psychological terms, it means that the purpose or meaning of human existence must point to something beyond ourselves. This self-surpassing quality or effort is what generally we call *self-transcendence.* By it we mean the challenge to reach beyond ourselves, to desire more than we have, and in the process to become more than what we are.

But how can we surpass ourselves? At the same time that we sense this longing for transcendence, we fear that not only does our biological death seem to spell our individual psychological death as individuals, but on top of that most indications are that all human life, along with our planet, the solar system, and even the universe, will eventually come to a dead end. Does this spell the end of human evolution or of existence itself? Thus in terms of the human desire for self-transcendence the question is: Is there anything, or *anyone* beside ourselves, on which we can place our hopes? Or to put it another way: How can there be self-transcendence without there being a transcendent meaning beyond that which we make up in our own minds?

This is the issue that ultimately confronts all questions about meaning and our hopes for fulfillment. Is there an "ultimate" or lasting meaning to our existence—or to all existence? The only answer to that question, according to Frankl, is to be found in *"faith"* which is "trust in ultimate meaning"—which I take to be another way of saying that God exists.

Questions for Reflection and Discussion

1. Think of an example where "faith" of some sort made all the difference in achieving some goal. Can you recount something similar that has happened in your own life or in the life of someone you know?
2. What do you think of Frankl's criticism of the search for happiness? Can you think of examples where "the pursuit of happiness" didn't work, especially from your own life?
3. What would be your idea of "meaning" in your own life? How would this fulfillment differ from mere "pleasure"? Would fulfillment be the same as "self-actualization"— yes or no? If not, how?
4. In what way are faith and "ultimate meaning" bound up with each other? Need such a faith be "religious"?

2. The Meaning of Faith

Faith is the state of being ultimately concerned. . . .
If it lays claim to ultimacy it demands total sur-
render of him who accepts this claim, and it promises total fulfillment.

Paul Tillich, *The Dynamics of Faith*

Those brought up with a more traditional Christian outlook on faith may have been surprised a bit by Frankl's
description of faith as "trust in ultimate meaning," just as
many may feel somewhat uneasy with theologian Paul Tillich's interpretation of faith as "ultimate concern." This un-
easiness is understandable. No doubt any faith worth consideration will begin with such concern, but hadn't there ought
to be much more to it than that? Doesn't Frankl's "trust"
even imply more? I agree. But before we can really delve
into the matter further, we have to arrive at some common
understanding or working definition of the word "faith."

For example, in a recent Gallup poll, taken at the re-
quest of the Religious Education Association of the United
States and Canada (see The Gallup Organization, Inc., *Faith
Development in the Adult Life Cycle,* Module 1), some 1,042
people were asked, among other things, to choose between
four different "definitions" of faith. A full fifty-one percent
of those who answered felt that "a relationship with God"
best described what they meant by faith. Twenty percent
thought of faith as "finding a meaning in life." Another nineteen percent understood faith to mean "a set of beliefs," but
only four percent associated faith as necessarily involving
"membership in a church or synagogue." (Of the remainder,
five percent had no answer to the question and a slim one
percent declared that faith was not meaningful as far as they
were concerned.)

Given these various ideas about what faith means to people today, it seems only logical to try to trace the reason for such a wide variety of opinions. To do this, I'm going to turn briefly to the work of a modern Catholic theologian, Avery Dulles, S.J.

Models of Faith

In his essay, "The Changing Forms of Faith" (see A. Dulles, *The Survival of Dogma,* pp. 17–31) Dulles gives us what amounts to seven variations in the understanding of the word faith down through history.

(1) *'Emunah* in the Hebrew scriptural sense denotes what we generally think of as *faithfulness* or "loyalty" or "steadfastness" today. This faith, however, has to be understood primarily in the context of God's faithfulness to his covenant or promises to his chosen people—thus their fidelity to God in return.

(2) *Pistis* in the New Testament, in view of its background in the Hebrew scriptures, includes this same idea of God's faithfulness to his promises and our faithfulness in return. But now this faithfulness has a new focus, and particularly in the synoptic gospels (Matthew, Mark, and Luke) the term *pistis* or "faith" means a *loving trust* in God's power working through Jesus. There is, however, a further development in a doctrinal direction in the various other New Testament writings, particularly the later Pauline "pastoral" epistles.

(3) *Early Christian* faith emphasized the *enlightenment* of humanity that was made possible through the revelation of Christ. In a sense, this early Christian understanding of faith was a continuation and expansion of the idea of faith already found in the gospel of John where Jesus is depicted as the "truth" and the "light of the world." This emphasis on "enlightenment" was highlighted by the then common reference to baptism as "illumination" and could be best un-

derstood in St. Augustine's famous phrase "I believe so that I may understand."

(4) *Medieval* faith continued the early Christian tradition, but with an increased emphasis on the body of *doctrine* or so-called "deposit of faith" that did not so much enlighten or expand the possibilities of human knowledge, but entirely surpasses it. Yet paradoxically, the scholastic theologians also subjected this doctrine to the scrutiny of human logic to a degree unheard of before and scarcely rivaled since. It was almost as if they were trying to turn Augustine's saying upside down or inside out and make every belief fully explainable by human reason.

(5) *Reformation* (*Protestant*) faith represents a strong reaction to the excesses of the later medieval scholars. The reformers, especially Luther, stressed faith as being primarily a complete *trust* in the saving *grace* earned by Christ on the cross. For this, Luther relied primarily on St. Paul's epistle to the Romans (as well as the epistle to the Galatians) where Paul reacts strongly against the Pharisees' notion of faith as mostly a matter of a painstaking keeping of the ancient law. To various degrees, all the reformation churches adopted Luther's motto of "Scripture alone, Faith alone, Grace alone."

(6) The *Catholic counter-reformation* stressed faith as the adherence to the "deposit of faith" (as understood by medieval theology) but with the old emphasis on understanding replaced by a new emphasis on *acceptance* of the church's teaching *authority* (not just that of the Bible alone), along with the performance of good works (against reliance on "grace alone"). This same approach was stressed again, but with renewed emphasis on the "reasonableness" of faith, at the First Vatican Council in 1870 to combat the rise of the modern sciences and the growing "modernist" ideas that faith is an irrational human "sentiment" or expression of a "religious impulse." But the earlier counter-reform em-

phasis on authority expressed at the Council of Trent still comes out on top even in the Vatican I statement used as the model of our old catechism definition:

> Faith is that supernatural virtue by which, through the help of God and through the assistance of His Grace, we believe what He has revealed to be true, not [on account of] the intrinsic truth perceived by the natural light of reason, but because of the authority of God Himself, the Revealer, who can neither deceive or be deceived (Session 3, Chapter 3).

(7) *Existential* faith, much discussed in our time, stresses the "leap of faith" or act of trust in God. It is not unlike Luther's idea of faith, but without his certainty in the infallibility of the Bible and with a strong emphasis on a *commitment* to human betterment that is not so evident from complete reliance on "grace alone."

Since the time of World War II, the lived experience of faith, even for Catholics, has shifted more and more in this "existentialist" direction. Vatican II, although endorsing the definition of faith given at Vatican I, has taken a more favorable view of the non-rational "fideism" that Vatican I so feared. This "religious sense" or impulse has, to some extent, been recognized and reunderstood more positively by the theologians and bishops of Vatican II as being at the core of the human quest. This quest is, even in the atheistic dreams of a materialistic paradise, a testimony to the unseen work of the Holy Spirit drawing the human soul to God (see "The Church in the Modern World," especially sections 10 and 22). If such existential longings are not "faith" in any actual sense of the word, they are the soil in which the seeds of faith can be planted, take root, and grow. To the precisely nuanced definition of Vatican I, the fathers of Vatican II place an additional emphasis, not so much on an obedience to the teaching of the church, but on an obedience to the impulse or grace of faith itself, "*the obedience of faith . . .* by which a man commits his whole self freely to God" (Vatican II, "Constitution on Divine Revelation," Section 5).

Before passing on from this historical overview of the various meanings of faith, I think we should also have a look at the one spot in the New Testament where something of a definition of faith is given. "Faith," says the writer of the epistle to the Hebrews (11:1), "is confident assurance concerning what we hope for, the conviction about things we do not see" (*The New American Bible* translation). *The New Jerusalem Bible,* on the other hand, translates this passage as: "Only faith can guarantee the blessings that we hope for, or prove the existence of the realities that remain unseen."

If the basic meaning of these two versions may seem close, the precise translation of the key words, *hypostasis* and *elegchos,* are the subject of much debate. If some, like *The Jerusalem Bible* translators, see them better translated as "guarantee" and "proof," others, as in the *New American* translation, understand them in less objective terms and more descriptive of the believer's state of mind. In terms of the models of faith given above, what we have here is a clash between what seems to be a Catholic emphasis on objective content (*what* is believed) and a Protestant emphasis on confidence (or *how* we believe). Yet both are Catholic translations of the Bible. But given the general context of the rest of the chapter (the ancient Hebrew patriarchs as examples of faith) it is clear that the author sees faith and hope as a single piece unfolding in time: past promise as leading to future fulfillment, faith as the ground of hope. (See Myles M. Bourke on "The Epistle to the Hebrews" in *The Jerome Biblical Commentary,* 61:62.)

It is obvious from all the above that the term "faith" can mean a multitude of things to many different people. If you doubt this, just look up the word in a modern dictionary. But part of the confusion also comes from the similar uses of another word, "belief." Wilfred Cantwell Smith, in his scholarly study *Faith and Belief,* has shown how the original English meaning of the word "believe" meant to "give one's love" to someone or something, particularly in the sense of pledging one's allegiance to the object of that love. This original meaning of "believe" can be traced to a common Germanic root word from which the modern German *lieb* or "love" takes its same origin. So in English, at least, "believe" should mean something very sacred and powerful. Unfortunately, the modern use of the word often means just the opposite, and we often end up using the word to describe any opinion regarding any matter that suits our fancy, even going so far as to say which team we "believe" will win the next world series.

As a practical note, I should say at this point that in this book I will try to restrict my use of the word "belief" to the contents or convictions that we hold in faith, even while occasionally using the verb "believe" to describe the *act* of faith, hoping that some of the ancient power of this word will sink in with its emphasis on a *loving* trust in and faithfulness to God. But on the whole, I think the time has come to try to gather in all these approaches to the meaning of faith into one basic understanding that takes in all these points of view. To do so would help us to arrive at a dynamic understanding of faith.

The Anatomy of Faith

Looking at the dictionary definitions as well as the various understandings of faith down through history, and even recent opinion polls, it is possible to see *three* basic meanings.

First, faith can mean *commitment,* fidelity, or allegiance; this is what the polls indicate that most people today mean by "faith." This meaning centers on the *act* of believing or having faith. Dulles calls this the "subjective" aspect or pole of faith, the personal element that we as responsible, deciding individuals bring into this relationship with God and ultimate truth.

Second, faith can also mean the *contents* or the system of beliefs that we speak of as a "religion." Dulles calls this the "objective" aspect or the pole that centers on *what* we believe. This is the part that Catholics and other Christians who lay great stress on doctrine sometimes speak of as "*the* faith." I will generally call this aspect the *conviction* of faith or "faith convictions"—that is, the things that we are convinced are the ultimate truth.

Finally, by "faith" people also mean a certain quality in their lives that involves a sense of optimism, or trust, or, if I may use a word based on the Latin word for faith (*fides*), a certain kind of *confidence*. It is also the meaning that has caused the greatest amount of confusion and misunderstanding about the nature of faith.

But I think I see something else. Recall the diagram that we saw in the last chapter, the one based on Viktor Frankl's. There we saw an upside down right-angled triangle with the agent-self at the bottom, and at the top-left corner, where the right-angle is formed, "meaning." Then off to the right side, "happiness" or "fulfillment." But we also learned, from elsewhere in Frankl's writings, that "religion is the search for ultimate meaning" and that "faith is trust in ultimate meaning."

Now, if we think of "ultimate meaning" as referring to the *objective* aspect of faith (which I prefer to call "conviction"), while the "search" part refers to our *subjective* "commitment" to truth, then I think we can take Frankl's description of faith as "trust" (or as I would term it, "confidence"), fit it into the third slot, and come up with this picture:

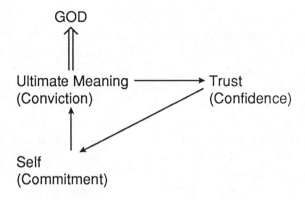

Just from comparing this diagram with the earlier one in the previous chapter, I think it is obvious why there is so much confusion about "faith" and why this third understanding of the word as "trust" or "confidence" has caused so many problems. As soon as we think of faith in terms of trust or confidence (the upper right of the diagram) we must also be led to the conclusion that this type of "faith" cannot be directly sought or achieved, or produced on command. It is, like "happiness" or "fulfillment" in Frankl's basic scheme, something that cannot be successfully "pursued" but can only *"ensue"*—it can only result as the *by-product* of the willing commitment of self to the ultimate meaning or truth.

This is why Frankl wrote in the new preface to his book, *The Unconscious God,* that faith, in the sense of a "will to believe," cannot be produced. Frankl is very clear about this. As he tells us, "there are certain activities that simply cannot be commanded," among them "the triad, faith, hope and love."

Why did he say this? It should be obvious if the emphasis is put on the "trust" in his definition of faith as "trust in ultimate meaning." If "religion is the search for ultimate meaning" (parallel to his "will to meaning" in the first diagram) then the present happiness or fulfillment of faith which is experienced as "confidence"—which I prefer to think of as the *"security"* of faith—can only come as a by-product of the search for greater or "ultimate" meaning.

From this we must conclude that the search for confidence or security for its own sake in the guise of religious faith is no less selfish than any other search for pleasure, power for its (or our) own sake nor any less futile than the quest for pleasure, happiness or fulfillment. It can't come to us this way. To attempt it is to defy the psychological laws of nature. Thought of in terms of baseball (but in this case involving a triangle rather than a "diamond"), we simply cannot get from home-base (self) and back (with the prize of happiness or fulfillment) without passing through first base first—a "meaning" greater than self. The confident security of faith (second base) can only "ensue." It can't be "pursued" directly, or if we do, we will commit a major error. If so, the result will turn out to be something less than faith in God. Faith, especially in this sense of "confidence," is always a gift, or, in biblical terms, a grace or "charism."

Faith, Hope, and Love

If faith is, in biblical and especially gospel terms, a loving trust, it is also a demanding one. If union with the God who is love is the only true "object" of our faith, it is only through the love of God, as God has first loved us, that faith in God or hope for ourselves is possible. As Cardinal Newman once put it: "It is love that makes faith, not faith love."

Newman's remark, I suggest, should prompt us to rethink the relationship between faith, hope, and love on the basis of the threefold understanding of faith as we have adapted it to Frankl's scheme. Personally, I've always found it particularly difficult to distinguish between faith and hope. As a "definition," the description of faith given in the epistle to the Hebrews as "confident assurance of things hoped for . . ." does not seem to clarify matters much. Nowadays it has often been said that in the face of uncertainty, hope has replaced faith as the major expression of religious consciousness. This may very well be true. But is it an adequate replacement?

I do not believe so, for if we were to take hope simply as our *future* expectations, we must ask what our *present* grounds are for such hope. The only answer can be the conviction we have that because something is *already* the case (for example, the resurrection of Jesus Christ), that what is *not yet* (in this example, our own "resurrection" to eternal life) is surely to come about. In other words, only the *contents* of faith, or faith understood from the viewpoint of "conviction," can bring about that "assurance of things hoped for" that we think of as the *confidence* of faith.

On the other hand, if we follow Newman's theological insight that love alone can account for faith, then we have to conclude that not only does God's love alone make faith possible, but also that our own *commitment* as an act of love is the psychological starting point of faith. Without this loving commitment and the *risk* it entails, no faith convictions are possible, nor can the *security* it promises possibly come about.

Start at the other end of the process, and everything comes out just the reverse. Confidence or security pursued for its own sake will fabricate contents to suit its own whims —which is the essence of idolatry—and this in turn will reinforce an egotistic self-love.

In basic human terms, there is no better analogy for the dynamics of faith (and hope and love as well) than its parallel in marriage. The biblical prophets knew this well—for them idolatry was the same as "adultery." Fundamentally, the commitment that marriage entails is always fraught with risk. True, if a person marries for money or for prestige, for security, or any other self-gratifying reason we may think of, there is risk as well, but when such marriages turn out to be a disaster or loveless at best, we all know why and condemn such persons for their foolishness. We may (or may not) feel sorry for them, but we are hardly surprised at the result. Only *commitment* "for better or for worse," to the other person "for richer or poorer, in sickness and in health" (in other words, not for one's money, not for one's looks), irrevocably "until death do them part" will do. Anything less than this commitment is not only a formula for disaster, but is "invalid" from the start.

So too with the commitment of faith, except for one big difference. God as the "other" in this partnership is *the* person or partner who will never fail. Thus we need never worry about our ultimate security. Our confidence, granted the sincerity of our commitment, is guaranteed. But the question remains: If faith (and hope) are produced by love, still how does love come to be?

If Frankl, from the psychological point of view, spoke of "faith, hope and love" as all being equally incapable of being produced on command, there are even deeper theological reasons for doing so. I think many will recognize this "triad" as being the three "theological virtues" as described by St. Paul (see 1 Corinthians 13:8–13). They have been termed such in Christian tradition because not only their final goal, but their origin as well, is in God—as distinguished from the four "cardinal" or pivotal moral virtues of prudence, justice, temperance, and fortitude, which have our own moral perfection as their primary aim.

So this means that when it comes to love—just as with faith and hope—although our ability to love is partly a matter of our own openness to love, we in no way can produce the results, as it were, by "pulling on our own boot straps." The same goes for our search for meaning. True, we can prepare ourselves by searching for that ultimate truth or meaning that we call "God." But if this committed search for meaning depends, to a large extent, on ourselves, theologians have long argued that even this beginning is an effect of God's grace working in us. So if arriving at that ultimate meaning or truth is what we mean by "believing," neither can this be successfully produced on command.

On the other hand, if it is true, as St. Augustine said, that "no one can be forced to believe," then I would add that not even God can force us to believe, nor for that matter can anyone force himself or herself to believe. At best we can only put ourselves at the disposal of God's grace.

So what all this comes down to is to say (with Newman) that the beginning of faith is the effect of a twofold love: first, God's love for us, and, second, our love for God. True, that love that we express for God at this beginning stage will be largely incoherent if not outright confused, since we do not yet "know" God. At best, it may be only a firm *commitment* to seek the truth over all else—but even that is enough to explain why Vatican II commends even those atheists who commit themselves to the betterment of this world as instruments of God's will. On the other hand, those who claim to know God and yet refuse to share in the works of God's redemptive love—can we really say they have "faith" in any meaningful sense? It would hardly seem so.

So what about the *object* or goal of faith? This is where the theological impact of Frankl's psychological truth is even more evident. Not only is it a case of where the security provided by faith cannot be successfully pursued as *the* goal of faith, but neither can the convictions or contents of faith be the object as well. This is why, in my second diagram, the "conviction" or "ultimate meaning" (upper left-hand corner of the triangle) really points (using a double arrow) beyond the triangle toward God. Our convictions or beliefs that form the intellectual contents of our faith, our "creeds" as we term them, are, in the end, "symbols"—they are attempts, in human language, to describe a reality that far exceeds our limited grasp. The closer we come to God in love the more inadequate these words become. The easily recited but often puzzling formulas of faith veil an ever deeper mystery. We must never imagine that we have "defined" (which is "to set limits to") God.

So too the same warning must be said about *hope;* it simply can't be produced by joining some ecclesiastical equivalent of the "Optimists' Club." The theological virtue of hope is, in some aspects, simply that part of faith that we call "confidence" and, as such, is that part of faith which least of all can be produced by us upon command. It can only come to us through that faith which is born from love. Any attempt to manufacture this hope through purely human means is bound to fail. Frankl (following St. Paul) may have spoken of the "triad" of "faith, hope and love" in that order—with love alone remaining when all is said and done—but the fact is that in terms of our ability or empowerment to have faith and hope, we must begin with love.

So, in a way, it all begins and ends in love. But it is here that the major problem with faith (and hope and love) begins—in our love of whom or what?

Self-love may be the psychological pre-condition (if not the theological limit) of our love for others; at the very least we must "love our neighbor as ourselves." For how can we love unless we first feel loved? Yet no such stipulation is set for our love of God. Instead, we are told that we must love God "with all your heart, with all your soul, and with all your mind," and that is "the first and the greatest of the commandments" (see Mt 22:37, also Dt 6:5 and Lev 19:18). So, theologically speaking, all love (even love for neighbor) ultimately must be included in and transformed by the love of God. As St. Augustine, who certainly knew his share of human loves, once said: "Our hearts were made for you, Lord, and they will not rest until they rest in you." This is certainly true of any self-love, however necessary that self-love be.

Thus Frankl's warning against the attempt to command faith, hope and love is warning against what is an expression of a "manipulative approach" in which the activities would become an end in themselves, and, in so doing, lose sight of their main objective. Faith, hope, and love are " 'intentional' acts or activities"—that is to say that they *in-tend* or "tend-to" their own proper objective, which is God (see Frankl, *The Unconscious God,* p. 14).

But why would a person attempt to manipulate or conjure up faith or hope or love in such a manner? Obviously because he or she hopes to get something out of it. So what we see is a subtle—or sometimes not so subtle—enthronement of our own personal needs as the real motivation for our believing, our hoping or our loving. Instead of being "theological virtues" in the full sense of being *theo-centric* or "God-centered," what we would have would be really an *ego-centric* striving posing as the quest for God. The so-called "theological virtues" are such not merely because they are a grace or gift of God, or because their only proper object or goal is God, but also because when truly possessed by a human being, the principal motivation is "for" or "for the sake of" God.

Thus faith cannot be simply a "belief in faith" as something good for us; rather it has to be a belief in God as the *ultimate good* that transcends us. In the same way hope cannot be authentic unless it is something more than just a hope "for hope's sake"—that is to say, for our own security's sake. Only love can be for love's sake, and this is only because ultimately (according to the apostle John) "God is love" (1 Jn 4:8 and 16).

Is such love or such faith possible? Perhaps not all at once. Here we might turn back to our comparison with married love. Both our commitment to God as well as our commitment to another person must be a growing relationship. One reason for this is that our perception of the "other," to some extent, will inevitably change. And along with this changing perception, the relationship itself will change.

Very often, in our youth, the other person is perceived as a reflection of ourselves or, more exactly, as the ideal counterpart of what we aspire to be. This is natural, and not without profound implications. But we must be careful, for that "other" is also a person in his or her own right. To try to force that person to conform to our own expectations is a violation of that person's integrity or "otherness." The maturity of the relationship must not only involve a growing unity, but a growing individualization as well. It has been said that "true unity differentiates." Although a certain similarity is a foundation for unity, its perfection is to be found in complementarity, not in uniformity or sameness.

The same goes for our relationship with God. Just as with married love, which usually begins in the attraction of "eros" and blossoms into the love of friendship—unless the erotic element is unrestrained—so too love of God will often begin on a strong note of "what's in it for me?" But just as a marriage that involves a true mutuality will regularly demand real self-sacrifice, so too the attraction to God that has ripened into a true friendship will also demand that "he must grow greater, I must grow less" (Jn 3:30).

For such love the New Testament has a special word; it is *agape*, the unconditional, self-sacrificing love that is celebrated in the famous thirteenth chapter of St. Paul's first letter to the Corinthians. Such love, it is true, transcends merely human capabilities. It is, above all, a gift—which is why *agape* is often translated as "charity" (from the Greek *charis* for "gift" or "grace"). But this uniqueness must not stand as an excuse or reason for evasion of our call to respond to it. Instead it is a demand that we move beyond the limits of our own self-concern and self-love. Instead of expecting God to cater to our own wants, faith demands that we set aside all idols and that we "let God be God."

The life of faith, like the love from which it issues and in which it ends, must be gradually deepened and transformed. Confident trust will more and more be tested by a renewed demand for a loving commitment to the *works of faith*. As in a marriage, mere words or signs of affection, as nice and as reassuring as they may be, are not enough. As Margaret Farley, in her excellent book *Personal Commitments: Beginning, Keeping, Changing,* makes clear, commitments are neither mere predictions of the future nor simple resolutions made in behalf of one's self. On the contrary, commitment involves a "giving of one's word" or a promise that lays a claim on us over our future. Mere good intentions and enthusiasm are not enough. "Not everyone who says to me, 'Lord, Lord,' will enter the kingdom of heaven; but he who does the will of my Father in heaven shall enter the kingdom of heaven" (Mt 7:21).

Nor is self-determination enough either. Just as faith and hope require love for their beginning, and that even this love is something that depends on God who has first loved us (1 Jn 4:10), it should be obvious that in the end, when the life of faith has reached its zenith, the measure of our faith will be the purity and sincerity of our love (see 1 Cor 13:1–13). What I have to say in the chapters that follow will attempt to show what this means for us at each stage of life.

Questions for Reflection and Discussion

1. What has been your own understanding or "definition" of faith? Were you satisfied with it? Why or why not?
2. How does your understanding of faith fit into Frankl's scheme (see the diagram in this chapter), and what does this tell you about any difficulties you've had with faith?
3. How is faith undercut by the search for absolute certainty or security? Give some examples of "manipulative" religion.
4. Reflect on your own experience with "faith, hope and love" in life. How does human experience in these matters throw light on the theological insight (or the other way around)?

3. The Beginnings of Faith

> To live is to change, and to live perfectly means to
> have changed often.
>
> John Henry Newman

Although it is commonly said that "the faith" remains timeless or changeless, the *way* or the *life* of faith is a process—it is a living, moving thing. Like so much else in life, faith that fails to develop and grow soon atrophies and perhaps even dies. This is not simply true of our individual commitment to the life of faith, but it is also true of the understanding of faith's *contents* or our doctrinal *convictions.*

There is nothing new in this. The fifth century monk-scholar St. Vincent of Lerins, whose ideas greatly influenced Cardinal Newman, had written on the "growth," "development," and "progress" of doctrinal understanding. And Newman's famous 1845 *Essay on the Idea of the Development of Doctrine,* in turn, greatly influenced the Second Vatican Council which clearly affirmed the idea of "a growth in understanding of the realities and words which have been handed down" ("Constitution on Divine Revelation," section 8, paragraph 2).

But we can trace this notion of growth in faith back even further to the New Testament itself. Not only do admonitions for a greater faith, in the sense of loving trust, fill the gospels and the epistles, but we also have direct appeals for a growth in the knowledge and understanding of the faith. In the epistle to the Colossians the apostle speaks of his prayers "that through perfect wisdom and spiritual understanding you should reach the fullest knowledge of his will . . . until they [you] are rich in the assurance of their [your] complete understanding and have knowledge of the mystery of God in which all the jewels of wisdom and knowledge are hidden" (see Col 1:5 and 2:2–3). Obviously, then, the idea of growth and development in faith, both in one's understanding and commitment, as well as in "assurance" or confidence, should be a major concern in Christian life.

Yet, oddly enough, while much has been written down through the ages on the stages of growth of Christian love and holiness, little has been done precisely on the idea of growth in or stages of faith. Recently, to our good fortune, the situation has changed.

The Stages of Faith

Among the most well-known studies on the subject of growth in faith have been those of the American theologian and religious researcher James Fowler and his colleagues. (See James W. Fowler, *Stages of Faith: The Psychology of Human Development and the Quest for Meaning*, 1981.) Fowler tested his theories by means of a series of exhaustive interviews of persons from many walks of life. Since then, The Religious Education Association of the United States and Canada commissioned further testing, first (as mentioned in the previous chapter) through The Gallup Association by means of a telephone survey of over one thousand persons, and again through exhaustive interviews, similar to those used by Fowler, of forty-one persons who were selected as being representative of the range of variations found in the larger poll. (See Constance Leean, *Faith Development in the Adult Life Cycle*, Module 2.)

Fowler divides his stages of faith development into six or seven, depending upon whether one counts the earliest, beginning level as involving "faith" in any meaningful sense. In his first book he assigns numbers from 0 through 6 to what amount to seven stages, while in his more recent book *Becoming Adult: Becoming Christian* (1984) he speaks of seven levels, but avoids assigning numbers, although in a few other places the Roman numerals I–VII are used instead. Also, in this later book, Fowler changes the names of two stages, calling "undifferentiated" faith "primal faith" and "paradoxical-consolidative" faith "conjunctive faith." Frankly, I'm not too happy with most of his designations, and in time we will consider more simple labels. But for the meantime, I will list Fowler's stages (with both sets of numbers) as follows:

0 (I)   Undifferentiated (or Primal) Faith
1 (II)   Intuitive-Projective Faith
2 (III) Mythic-Literal Faith
3 (IV)   Synthetic-Conventional Faith
4 (V)   Individuative-Reflexive Faith
5 (VI)   Paradoxical-Consolidative (or Conjunctive) Faith
6 (VII) Universalizing Faith

We may well ask: What is the basis for saying that a person is in this or that stage of faith? If one studies the charts that accompany much of Fowler's work, one can see that he uses what amounts to seven basic criteria. We may at first wonder what they have to do with faith life, but it will become more evident as we look at each stage. To get an overall idea of what signs Fowler was paying most attention to, I've listed them as follows with a few comments (see also the chart in the Appendix):

a. Form of Logic (kind of thinking processes used)
b. Perspective Taking (how one relates to others)
c. Form of Moral Judgment (or why behave?)
d. Bounds of Social Awareness (who's going to care?)
e. Locus of Authority (who's in charge?)
f. Form of World Coherence or "Worldview"
g. Role of Symbols

Some of these items may appear to have little or nothing to do with faith, but if we were to study developmental psychology as Fowler has, we would find some of these things extremely revealing. For example, take the first—our "form of logic" or thinking process. In the earlier stages of childhood, reasoning, if it exists at all, has to be presented in very concrete terms, on the level of "apples and oranges" so to speak. Or take the last criterion, the role played by "symbol." It is obvious that the ability "to see through" the familiar term "Father" as applied to God is a critical factor for many persons, particularly during this period when many Christians are searching for a more comprehensive or inclusive understanding of God.

Several other things also should be said at this point about Fowler's "stages." One is that there can be a considerable amount of overlapping from one stage to another and that a person's ideas and attitudes in one or more categories may exhibit the characteristics of a faith stage that is either earlier, on the one hand, or more advanced, on the other, than the stage where he or she seems to generally be. Still, on the whole, it is typical of people to fall more or less consistently into one stage or another across the whole range of criteria.

Another thing, which should be obvious from his beginning attention to the type of reasoning and kind of world-view a person has, as well as the final consideration of the role that symbols take, is that Fowler's focus, although much concerned with the element of "commitment" in faith, is first of all focused on the intellectual contents or "convictions." And although he is not doing this to rate this or that set of beliefs—the Christian faith, or the Jewish faith, or whatever—still, it is clear that when such elements are considered along with those such as our understanding of authority, our view of our role in the world, and bounds or limits of social awareness, together all these factors have some bearing on our ability to relate to and cope with the world as it really is.

Put into other words—and we must try to make this as clear as possible—Fowler's stages do not claim to judge the sincerity of a person's faith, much less his or her moral goodness or holiness. One can, theoretically, be in an early stage of faith development, and still be a saint. This is particularly true when the person lives within a society that is predominantly operating within the same stage or level of faith. *Holiness,* which also can be described in terms of "human authenticity before God" or an "intensive" quality, can at least theoretically remain a "constant" through all faith and life stages. (See especially chapter seven of Daniel A. Helminiak's *Spiritual Development: An Interdisciplinary Study.*) Nevertheless, it can be strongly argued that the quality of this holiness suffers unless one's faith development is appropriate to one's life stage.

Finally, another problem exists regarding the typical age or level of maturity that these stages seem to imply. Fowler tries to avoid assigning appropriate or typical age brackets, yet it is quite obvious that the first three or four stages are quite predictable in terms of child development. Nevertheless, the "mythic-literal" faith that typifies school-age children, although it seems inappropriate to older persons, is quite common in certain segments of our population, especially in the "Bible Belt." In the next chapter we will have to pay particular attention to this peculiar American phenomenon.

But this in turn raises questions about the next level, the "conventional-synthetic" stage, which by definition, in that it is *conventional,* appears to be the *norm* (in the sense of "average") level of religious consciousness throughout the rest of American society. Typically, this stage begins in the early teenage years, and, if we are to believe the researchers, is apt to continue for the rest of most persons' lives. The fact that this "conventional" stage often persists is taken by some to be an indication that Fowler's whole idea is off-base, especially when it comes to the idea that there are "higher" forms of faith. But this objection hardly seems worthy of serious consideration unless one ignores the whole tradition of spiritual development and thinks of faith as some kind of take-it-or-leave-it "package deal" coming down to us out of the blue—obviously, I don't.

Aside from that, I think it is also clear that the progression through the higher stages of faith has a lot to do with one's psychological growth, but that maturity in this area often lags far behind one's chronological age. And conversely, the most that can be said here is that the more advanced stages are rarely, if ever, possible before a certain age is reached. Or if certain aspects of a more mature faith show themselves early on in life, one can hardly expect all the criteria of that stage to appear across the board. They rarely do so even in genuinely mature persons, so what can we expect when a younger person shows some of these characteristics except to say that this or that aspect of his or her thinking is "precocious" or even, to some extent, "premature"?

While many other criticisms have been leveled at Fowler's ideas, I don't think this is the place to deal with them. Most of them apply specifically to one or another of the stages, and we will consider each of them when the most appropriate time comes. What I would like to emphasize, however, is that my concern is not so much to familiarize the reader with each stage in all its details but rather to use each stage as the occasion to examine a typical example of the faith dynamic or process at work and to point out how and why the process of growth in faith can often be arrested or thrown off the tracks completely. To some extent Fowler's "stages" are merely like rungs on a ladder. I'm much more concerned with the upward movement of the feet of the person than I am with either the order or the number of the rungs. But first we must look at the first two steps.

"Undifferentiated" or Instinctive Faith

Fowler at first numbered this "undifferentiated" faith as "0" on his list, not regarding it as "faith" in any meaningful sense. Later on Fowler speaks of it as "primal faith," seeing it as more significant after all, and at least one chart outlining his stages counts it with the Roman numeral "I." This change, I think, seems to indicate a switch from a theological to a more psychological outlook on Fowler's part. But, as we shall soon see, these two aspects are very closely connected.

First, looked at from a theological perspective, "faith" at this stage is without any intellectual *conviction* or *commitment* as far as the infant is concerned. At most, the infant's "faith" is a feeling of *confidence* that is indistinguishable, hence "undifferentiated," from infantile trust. It is also, to this degree, "instinctive," at least in the broad sense of the term, since it grows almost automatically out of the initial experience of parent-child bonding—hence my preference for this latter term.

For these same reasons it is hard to see where we can speak of the infant during its first months or years of life as having "faith" in any real sense of the term—unless, of course, we appeal to the existence of some type of "infused" grace or potential faith held to come along with the sacrament of baptism. But this theological perspective carries with it certain psychological implications. This strong sacramental emphasis is based on the idea of God's "predestinating" grace, along with the idea that it is the church, as represented by the parents and "godparents," that supplies the faith commitment that cannot, at this stage, be given by the child.

Although this explanation may deepen our theological appreciation of the *gift* of faith, in other ways it only seems to further complicate the question. How can the personally chosen "rebirth" which baptism is supposed to signify (according to the theologies of St. John and St. Paul) be accomplished "by proxy," as it were? Such an idea seems completely alien to one of the earliest Christian theologians, St. Justin Martyr, who wrote:

> . . . our first birth took place without our knowledge or consent. . . . So if we were not to remain children of necessity and ignorance, we needed a new birth of which we ourselves would be conscious, and which would be the result of our own free choice (*First Apology in Defense of the Christians*, Chap. 61).

Theologically speaking, the problem has never been fully resolved. The early church took some centuries to reach the point where infant baptism became widely accepted, and often it seems that the theology to explain why only appeared sometime later. As often happens in history, and as the saying goes, "*lex orandi, lex credendi*" (the "law of prayer [is] the law of belief"), or, to put it another way, theory follows practice. Aside from the earliest times, when most people came into the church by way of adult conversions, the majority of Christians down through history have baptized their infants, but many others, finding the theological justifications at best shaky, have repudiated the practice.

For myself, I must say that while I believe the tradition allows for *valid* infant baptism, the theological teaching that a sacrament is an *effective* sign raises the question as to whether or not such baptisms are desirable under many situations, which is to ask if under some conditions the granting of baptism to an infant does not turn out to be a barrier instead of a help to future faith. Indeed, Roman Catholic canon law itself deems such infant baptism *illicit* when certain conditions, like a stable Christian home-life, or an acceptable substitute for it, cannot be met.

So the real focus of the conflict at this stage revolves perhaps not so much around the child as the parents and other concerned persons. The sacramental induction of the child into the Christian community, along with a poor understanding of scripture and a resulting theology that often was distorted in its popular presentation, too often has been seen as a guarantee of salvation that was so automatic as to relieve the parents and godparents of any further obligations or serious efforts toward bringing the child up in the faith. Baptism has been too often thought of as a "ticket to heaven" instead of a vocation to Christian witness and responsibility. This mentality has had its major expression in the almost automatic conferring of infant baptism, often against the regulations of church law. A new caution, derived from long-standing practices in the mission fields and adapted to the situation of "cultural Christianity," has recently worked its way into enlightened pastoral practice and revised liturgical rites.

Leaving aside the question of the desirability of baptism at this stage in life, even at this "undifferentiated" level there is an important factor affecting the growth of faith in the infant soon to become a young child. If we are to believe developmental psychologists there is a critical factor of "faith"—in the sense of *trust*—that has to be considered. Most authorities seem to agree that unless, during these critical months of infant development, the child can consistently depend on the parents' expression of love and care, there will later appear in the child's psychological makeup a profound lack of confidence in persons and in the world at large. A baby who cries for help, for food, or simply to have its diapers changed, and whose cries bring no response, could very well grow up to become a distrustful and suspicious person—a person who has little or no instinctive foundation for belief in a loving God.

When we speculate on the origins of the *security* needs

that so often cripple growth in faith, we can hardly overlook the effects that may be caused by frustrated security needs at this earliest stage of life. If, in some sense, the life of the young infant is a continuation of that experienced in the womb despite the traumatic interruption of being born, in the same way the faith that should someday appear in the developing person is also the continuation of the trust engendered during these earliest months of life. If the child without trust is, in some way, a child who has never been fully born, who has not yet successfully negotiated the course from the complete dependency of the womb through the incipient independence of birth, so too the "man of little [or no] faith" may have the roots of his inadequacy in the absence or breakdown of infant trust.

As for the *risk* factor in this stage of faith, I think we are caught between the horns of a dilemma. On the one hand, how do we cope with the *risk* that infant baptism will become practically meaningless to the person who has received it at this beginning stage of life or that its impact will actually turn out to be negative should the fact of one's having been baptized become too closely associated with a less than Christian example given by one's parents?

On the other hand, the growing tendency of parents to put off their children's baptism has its risks as well—both for parent and child. Too often the argument that "we believe it is best to wait till our children can decide for themselves" masks indifference on the parents' part which will surely rub off onto their children as well. The fact is that children will sooner or later decide for themselves, but, in the absence of any religious concern by the parents, the children's "decision" will be to consider faith irrelevant to life. To send children off on this course is to deprive them of any deep sense of meaning in life and to pave the way for future unhappiness. The "existential neurosis" that Frankl deemed endemic in the modern world is first and foremost the product of a culture that has lost its religious foundations. I would suggest that Fowler's elevation of this stage from 0 to I is a sign of the seriousness of this risk.

This is another reason why I prefer to think of this same stage as *instinctive* rather than "undifferentiated" faith. This older term of Fowler's is too close to suggesting the word "indifferent," and I think that our brief discussion of the importance of infant "trust"—as well as the tricky issue of infant baptism—indicates that indifference to this risk is the last thing we can afford.

Intuitive Faith

Like the earliest "instinctive" faith, the "faith" typical of the next stage, that of the pre-school child, is also, to a large degree, "undifferentiated" from simple trust in one's parents or other significant persons in one's life. But the small child does begin to differentiate in the sense that the concept of God as a *significant other* begins to appear in the child's consciousness. True, the child's ideas of God may be highly magical or greatly confused—what pastor has not had the experience of being identified as "God" by a small child, especially after being told by parents that the church is "God's house" and the pastor dramatically appears in front in flowing robes? At best, the young child's views of the world at this stage are still somewhat disconnected and episodic, causal relationships are fuzzy, and morality is apt to be strictly a business of simple punishment and reward.

We should pay particular attention to the fact that at this second stage, certain words may take on very special, even "loaded," significance. To call God "Father" is certainly a matter of grave importance, particularly when we realize that to do so will almost automatically cause the child to look to his or her father as the model for his or her ideas of God. This should make us very careful about our word choices—for example, what is the small child who views Saturday morning's animated TV cartoon to make of some people's habit of referring to God's Holy Spirit as the Holy "Ghost"?

At this stage, we might say that "faith," besides being confused with trust in the parent and largely a *projection* of that same trust toward this super-parent called God, may also manifest certain "totemic" qualities. Security, as is to be expected, continues to be primarily invested in the presence of the parent, but sometimes it becomes also identified with certain objects—a teddy bear or other toy, maybe an old blanket or certain piece of clothing.

Maybe it is a bit harsh to unduly criticize the foibles of adult believers that seem to mimic or prolong such behavior, but the persistence of totemistic elements in otherwise more sophisticated stages of belief is disconcerting. Granted that symbols play an important function in all stages of religion, still it is obvious that certain symbols or objects, particularly when they are *this* or *that* particular medal, cross, rosary, etc., and not simply one similar to it, can be looked upon more as good luck charms or amulets instead of reminders to lead us to prayer, although certain sentimental attachments may explain part of this situation. But similar attitudes sometimes attach themselves to certain prayer formulas; they become invested with the qualities of incantations used to ward off bad luck or disaster. In this respect I can't say I've been much impressed with those boxers who make a sign of the cross before embarking on their mayhem. Too often such rituals, in particular, become a compulsive matter, an either/or proposition—either I do this and I will be OK, or if I don't I'll be punished. So-called religious "chain letters" are instructive in this regard; rarely are they simply requests for prayer, but often betray their obsessive-compulsive characteristics by ending with a threat.

The reward/punishment level of morality that continues into this stage also manifests its pathological potentials when it is extended later into life. The condition known as "scrupulosity," a sort of religious hypochondria, probably has its psychological roots in this level of thinking. Things are perceived as right or wrong not so much because of some intrinsic reasonableness, but because rewards and penalties appear to have been arbitrarily attached to certain actions. The scrupulous person finds himself or herself constantly condemned by his or her conscience almost regardless of inner intention, just as for the hypochondriac, the world is filled with germs waiting for the chance to do them in. We might find here also a kindredness between various food and health fads and religious neurosis, so much so that one suspects that the hygienic obsession is partly a manifestation of suppressed religious consciousness. So too for the scrupulous, the world, even the religious world, and, even more, their own minds, are filled with thousands of temptations, sins (either acted out or imagined) that leave them in a state of mental anguish and exhaustion.

I focus especially on this particular miscarriage of the faith process not because it is common—although it was more common when morality was taught exclusively in terms of commandments and church regulations—but because it illustrates more dramatically than the other characteristics of this faith level the struggle involved between security and risk. Scrupulous persons, despite their religious preoccupation, seem to be persons of very little faith. Even if they were guilty of even a fraction of the sins they imagine themselves to be, they really do not trust God to forgive them. They are unwilling to take the risk of faith and leave their salvation in the hands of God. Instead, they hanker after an impossible ritual *purity* (it is not insignificant that most such persons worry principally over sexuality) and rarely, if ever, will take a pastor's words of forgiveness or assurance to heart. They have to not only *know*—infallibly and without any doubt—that they are forgiven, but, even more, they have to *feel* forgiven as well.

The cure for such a condition does not come easy, either for scrupulous persons or for the unhappy pastor who tries to help them. It begins with trust, and most often, along with it, an authoritative command from someone they have begun to trust. In other words, it demands taking the *risk* of believing someone almost as unconditionally as if they were meeting God face to face. Only then, once such trust begins to bear fruit, can they be gradually brought around to a more reasonable and a more profound understanding of morality and religion. Whatever the hidden root cause of this condition—and it generally goes deeper than poor religious education—it is one hundred percent certain that ultimately its cure is to be found in faith. Erik Erikson, who in his psychobiography *Young Man Luther* depicts Martin Luther as having suffered greatly from this affliction, leans toward blaming Luther's overbearing father for his condition. In any case, Luther comes to mind as a good example of a religious leader who was driven to find his own answer in, and indeed to go on to expound a whole theology based primarily on, faith and trust in God's grace.

As for the other symptoms of faith being arrested at this level, I suspect that the corrective lies, to begin with, in correct religious education and perhaps even in liturgical reform. Superstitious use of religious objects and symbols has been an age-old problem, as the Hebrew scriptures well illustrate. But the current residue of such practices figures greatly where basic instruction in religion is inadequate and where there remain strong cultural overlays of former non-Christian or even polytheistic religions. The mentality seems to be that although one may believe in Jesus and the God of the Bible, still it never hurts to be on the safe or extra secure side by also placating whatever other gods, demons, or whatever may still be around. One can never be too sure about such things.

It should not surprise us that such mentalities still exist. Whole cultures still exist that practice religion in this frame of mind, and some of these cultures are even nominally Christian. The reasons are more fundamental than theology.

In primitive or largely sustenance-oriented cultures and economies, the main preoccupation in life is having enough to eat—an unpredictable business under such conditions. Religion is naturally centered, in its day to day prayer and ritual aspect, on making sure that there is food on the table. As a consequence, the practice of religion takes on a certain "manipulative" quality. Prayer is primarily a coaxing of the god or gods who tend to be stingy at times, and the intercession of other holy beings, demi-gods, angels, and saints is much cultivated. Charms and totemic objects are venerated. Taboos are feared and respected, and moral standards rarely apply when dealing with those outside ones own tribal group.

I paint this overdrawn and somewhat negative picture of so-called "primitive religion" not to come down hard on other societies and cultures—they also have their positive religious qualities, like a deep respect of nature as sacred—but to caricature what religion tends to become even in a modern civilization when there is an arrest of faith at this intuitive-projective level. The basic problem, aside from neurotic causes, as with severe problems like scrupulosity, or cultural limits (whether regional or educational), more generally lies in a basic lack of trust or faith in a loving God. In place of this God, we idolize whatever best insures security, whether it be the observance of a ritual, the superstitious and not just sentimental reliance on a medal, a prayer, or a vigil light, or, again, the scrupulous observance of misguided conscience. So too the religion-substitute protections of diet-fads and other hygienic obsessions. We might even add to our list the security-driven obsessions with laser-beaming mirrors aimed at outer space and other technological good-luck charms—the search for absolute security never ends.

The cure for such an arrest of faith development is, obviously, more—and more authentic—faith. But of course this is easier said than done. I have already prescribed some remedies for the scrupulous. And when it comes to primitive societies, I suppose one could always call for conversion to *true* religion and more education. But here I think we would miss the more obvious point. Missionaries for years now have realized that a Christian life or any life of real faith also demands a *human* life. "Grace builds upon nature" as the old theological adage has it. Today we see these same insights in a much more sophisticated and radical form in "liberation theology"—the only real difference is that the hungry people are now *risking* everything to bring this about. They are tired of waiting for our benevolence.

But what is the risk demanded of us? On the whole, especially when we are dealing with faith problems that have their origin on this "intuitive-projective" level of faith, but which I prefer to simply call "intuitive faith," our primary challenge is to overcome the false or distorted *images* of God or other aspects of religion which we may have acquired as a child. Indeed, so pervasive is the influence of our "images" or "pictures" on our faith life that Richard J. Sweeney calls this stage "Imaginative Faith" (see "How God Invites Us To Grow" in the *Catholic Update* series, October 1987). For example, a study made at the University of Michigan some years ago revealed that a majority of those identifying themselves as atheists also revealed problems with their relationship to their father. From my own pastoral experience I am almost equally convinced that many adult Catholics who have problems with their church may often turn out to have had some problem with their mother— hardly surprising considering the long-standing Catholic tradition of referring to "Holy Mother Church."

The risk then, for many, involves the pain, and sometimes the real trauma, of confronting often very distressing memories of childhood and allowing these to be healed. Often this can turn out to be a rather lengthy process, occasionally even involving the help of professional psychotherapy. But however one goes about it, the most essential ingredient of all will be the very risky feeling of "letting go" of our long-standing habits of self-insulation from or self-protective defenses against confrontation with these threatening images.

Less serious, but perhaps even more pervasive in its influence, is another "projection" from early childhood on our faith as adults. Here I am referring to the often repeated admonition that our faith should be as that of "little children"—trusting, accepting, and, most of all, it is claimed, unquestioning. Not only is this attitude a real hindrance to the growth of faith; it is, I venture to claim, a real distortion of the gospel as well. As we have seen, "faith," in the gospel context, means primarily a *loving trust.* Nor are we talking here about the existential *commitment* of faith, which demands real maturity. Here we are speaking about our appreciation for and understanding of the *convictions* of faith, which, as we have seen, St. Paul tells us must be continually deepened and strengthened. Besides, who asks more questions than the small child? It is precisely because a child implicitly trusts and believes that he or she is not afraid to ask all kinds of questions. It is often due to a put-down on the part of parents or later on by teachers, or even by pastors who distort the gospel in this way, to "pull rank" and shame people into conformity that much religious teaching is held in contempt.

Or to take another variation of this same problem—that caused by wrong or false religious teaching. Of course, this can happen at any age, but again the danger is greatest when false images and ideas are given to the small child. St. Augustine's own experience of being misled occurred when he was older, but he described the problem very graphically when he warned, over fifteen hundred years ago:

> [A]s usually happens, the person who has tried a bad doctor is afraid even to trust a good one; so it was with the health of my soul, which could not be

healed save by believing, and refused to be healed that way for fear of believing falsehood (*Confessions,* VI, 4).

Conclusion

If, in this introduction to the concept of "stages of faith," I have emphasized what is, especially in the case of the first stage, hardly faith in the proper, or at least full sense of the word, it is to underline the importance of good beginnings. The security needs of the infant and small child are demanding, and the corresponding risks and responsibilities fall primarily upon the parents and other educators in the faith. But what if these exemplars themselves are lacking in understanding or in consistency? If we are to "believe that we might understand," we need just as much to know how we come to faith as we understand our beliefs as such.

Questions for Reflection and Discussion

1. At what point in your life was your faith most challenged? Did your faith grow or diminish as a result of that challenge? How and why?
2. Does the idea of "stages" or "levels" of faith strike you as strange or not?
3. What were your earliest images of God? What most influenced these images?
4. What attitude were you taught regarding your own questions about faith?

4. Literal Faith

Those who have the faith of children will also have the troubles of children.

Robert Hugh Benson, *The Light Invisible*

If there is something to be said in favor of the simple faith or trust that is held to be typical of early childhood, Benson's warning should make us rather cautious when it comes to this next stage, which is most apt to occur in middle or late childhood. Fowler terms this stage "mythic-literal faith" but I prefer to call it (along with Richard J. Sweeney) simply "literal faith." Since these are the years that, roughly speaking, are covered by primary schooling, they are also important years of transition. Although the psychological changes corresponding to this faith stage are more or less automatic, there nevertheless are apt to be certain difficulties which, if not dealt with correctly, can greatly obstruct any future maturing of faith. When this happens, the resulting faith is more likely to turn out to be *childish* rather than "childlike." Further development into the stages that should normally follow becomes difficult if not impossible.

However, anything resembling a total blockage would only rarely happen in the case of the passage from "intuitive faith" to "literal faith." If there is any conflict here it is more likely that unresolved problems from the intuitive stage will pass into the later stages but will disrupt the chances of an orderly development. The result will be that certain aspects of these later stages will be bent out of shape. For example, the old problem of a neurotic scrupulosity, with its roots in the intuitive stage, will often recur in various forms in the stages that follow.

In much the same way, certain aspects of the literal faith of childhood will sometimes reappear in conventional faith, or, even more often, in some forms of the more individual or personal faith that we associate with "born again Christians" and other related types. In that case, what we often run across is that form of faith that is sometimes called "fundamentalism," and which often appears to be a regression to this earlier literal stage—a perplexing situation that might make one wonder if the whole faith development scheme proposed by Fowler is valid in the first place.

However, I feel that once Fowler's findings and his conclusions are understood in the light of Frankl's thought, not only is this seeming regression understandable, but it is even highly predictable under certain conditions. But before we attempt to understand this phenomenon, and the kind of "fundamentalism" it occasions, we have to first understand "literal faith" in its natural setting, which is childhood or, more specifically, the primary school years.

Myth and Belief

As we have seen, Fowler speaks of this stage as "mythic-literal faith." Unfortunately, the word "myth" has acquired an unsavory connotation in modern speech, generally equated with some sort of elaborate form of lie. But this should not excuse us from trying to understand the vital place that "myth" in the proper and original sense of the Greek word *mythos* (meaning a story, especially a sacred story) plays in religious consciousness and the evolution of human culture. And to do this we must reenter the world of the child, for the evolution of religious consciousness and consequently of human culture is in some way—if we are to follow the great British historian Arnold Toynbee who believed all human culture has religious roots—the childhood of the human race.

The thinking of the typical primary school child at first still operates much like that of the pre-school child. It is very much on the concrete, "apples and oranges" level. However, it has become much more realistic as opposed to magical and the fantastic. But abstractions—integers instead of apples— still are grasped with some difficulty, and *story,* whether fictional or historical, forms the matrix as well as the major vehicle of truth. The child cannot easily absorb abstract principles, but he or she can readily identify with the heroes and heroines of the past when they are presented not as part of the dry data of history but as living personalities within a panorama of colorful deeds. The child may not easily grasp the abstract principles of moral reasoning, but can readily identify what seems right or wrong in terms of loyalty and basic fairness.

The same is very much true of the "childhood" of whole civilizations or cultures. Stories are the preferred means of handing on cultural values. The Homeric epics of ancient Greece, the Bardic poetry of the Celts, the Norse sagas, the *Kalevala* of the Finns, the earliest *Vedas* of the Hindus—all of these are highly mythological, combining fanciful tales of gods and demons, legends about ancient heroes, vague memories of natural disasters, fateful battles, epic migrations, and genealogical pedigrees mixed with the anecdotes, both sad and joyful, that mark each people as special and give them a sense of their own destiny and self-worth.

Should we be at all surprised if the composition of the Bible has much in common with all this? Hardly not! For if it was to speak effectively to the people of the time in which it was first written, or to the people that came long before—realizing that much of the biblical material was passed on by means of an oral or spoken tradition long before it was written down—it had to be in the form that best reached them, that is, in the form of sacred story or myth. Can you imagine, for example, the confusion that would have happened if the author of the book of Genesis had attempted to describe the creation of the world in modern evolutionary terms? Not only would he have been trying to write in a modern scientific language which would have been completely unintelligible to his readers, he would have ended up in missing the main point of the whole story to begin with.

And that is the crucial question we must face: What is the point of these stories? To give information about the shape of the earth, which the Bible takes for granted is flat, with the sky or "heavens" like an upside-down bowl covering it? Or is it to tell us about how they were created? Genesis combines two stories to tell us about that. Or to tell us what exactly happened that long day when Joshua won his battle? (The Bible says the sun stood still—so do we have to conclude instead that the earth stopped spinning?) If we think that the Bible is trying to give us such information, we are missing the whole point. To quote a pun made by a very wise cardinal who was unfortunately not much listened to when the churchmen condemned Galileo for his revolutionary ideas: "The Bible was written to tell us how to go to heaven, not to tell us how the heavens go."

Unfortunately, many people continue to make this same mistake. Why is this so? To understand this, we have to understand something of how our minds work. All language—and language is the tool or the way by which we structure our thoughts—is *analogical,* that is, everything is, to some extent, compared to something else. If, for example, I was from the arctic tundras or some other treeless region and had never seen a tree, and asked you what a tree was like, you might answer that it was something like a bush, only a lot bigger. Or if someone asks what is meant by a "family tree," we press the analogy even further and compare common ancestors to a "trunk" and speak of "branches" of the family. So it is, to some degree, with all language. Another way of saying this is that all language is symbolic. Something, a word, a sound, a combination of letters (each letter itself is a symbol derived from a system of simple pictures of things), always stands for something else.

The more difficult it is to describe something or to think about it, the more we must employ analogy and symbol.

Now what could be more difficult to describe than God? We may think that this should be simple to do, but the fact is that all the religious thinkers, philosophers, and mystics, while they claim that God is supremely simple, also admit that all the human language in the world is incapable of describing God, or even of describing our relationship to God. So what do we do? We turn even more to symbol, and particularly to that kind of symbolic story that is called "myth."

But the reason for myth is not just because we are trying to describe the indescribable. Story, as I already said, is more easily remembered, especially by people who can't read. But stories also often turn out to be a more effective way of getting a point across. Thus Jesus himself made up little stories (parables) which by their frequent surprise endings were all the more effective in teaching a moral lesson than any rote memorizing of a commandment or law.

Finally, sometimes myth or story, by the sheer force of exaggeration, is all the more memorable. St. Jerome, the first officially appointed translator of the Bible into Latin, suspected that the book of Jonah was just such a fictional tall tale, a really "big fish story" in almost modern short-story form designed to teach a profound lesson about obeying God, even while it delights its audience. (It is my favorite story in the whole Bible—one can imagine the author's struggle to keep his sense of humor in check lest he scandalize his reading public who by that time probably thought all sacred literature had to be solemn.)

However, delightful and natural as this all may be, myth does present problems, especially for modern people. Although children are most able to delight in story and not worry too much about whether or not all these things are factually "true," as we begin to lose the innocence of childhood—and this loss seems to begin ever earlier in modern times—we begin to question about the factualness of these tales. Did these things *really* happen? Or did they happen in the way they are described? In a word, are they really *true*?

One of the best, even if rather flippant, definitions of "myth" is "a truth that never happened." That is to say these stories contain profound truths about the nature of things, about ourselves, and about God, but do so in story form without pinpointing a time in history or a location where we could expect to find hard evidence—unlike the people who keep looking for the wreck of Noah's ark. The clue very often is an almost timeless time frame often expressed as "In the beginning . . ." (in other words, *before* all time began) or alternately "Once upon a time . . ." (which means that it could have happened, or still can happen, *any* time). In still others, the time reference is to a particular point, maybe a crisis point in history, but one that is defined more by human development rather than by the passage of years—for example, the "tower of Babel" story in Genesis.

All this may be very interesting, but the point is this. Although the "mythic" component of this faith stage is a very natural one, it also presents a major problem. Initially, there is generally little or no difficulty with myth because the small child has no need to distinguish between the story element and the truth it contains—or as Marshall McLuhan put it, "the medium is the message." But send a child to school and what happens? The effect is much the same as when a child is driven downtown in mid-December and sees a red-suited, white-bearded man on every other street corner, and the parent has to begin to separate the truth (the spirit of giving) from the "Santa Claus" myth. And the task is not always easy. It may be of some help to know that there once was an actual St. Nicholas who was known for his generosity to poor families, but very little historical data is available and our best efforts are frustrated by the crass commercialism that lays great store on keeping visions of reindeer and "sugar-plums" dancing in children's heads.

We are faced with a similar problem when it comes to the myths found in the Bible. The story of creation in Genesis is vivid and attractive, and highly effective in getting across the main point—that God is the creator of everything there is and everything God created is good. But schools soon teach us that the earth is round, that it circles the sun, and that the earth is at least five billion years old, and that most likely human life began evolving from lower forms only a few million years ago. So most likely the clash between evolutionary science and the natural, naive literal understanding of the sacred stories will precipitate at least a minor "crisis of faith" even long before junior high. So unless a child is prepared by his or her parents and teachers to see the major point of these stories, some real difficulty may be experienced in separating the factual content from the story forms that the ancients found to be the most expressive way of conveying the deeper truths. Failure to do so may set the stage for a much more serious crisis of, or even loss of, faith in later years. The late Swiss theologian Karl Rahner even went so far as to suggest that some of these biblical stories which form the grist of many Sunday school classes *not* be told to children until they are of sufficient age to distinguish between truths and the mytho-poetic story forms that contain them (see *The Practice of the Faith: A Handbook of Contemporary Spirituality*, pp. 124–25).

Either that, or a person may be driven into an arrestment of faith development that will lead to a kind of religion that is almost certain to be "fundamentalistic" in the most literal sense. When this happens, a person takes nearly everything written in the scriptures at face value as the literal truth. The most obviously mythic literary forms in the Bible, such as those in the first ten chapters of Genesis, are taken as historical and even quasi-scientific accounts in a way that most likely even the original author(s) and editors would have found puzzling, if not ludicrous. This is not to say that the first hearers and readers of these stories might not have taken them literally, but one may suspect that people in these early civilizations also had a certain sixth sense that made the main point of these tales obvious and that they didn't worry much about the details of the story line. (We can sense this from the way that the various stories, often with conflicting versions, are set side by side or dovetailed together in the Bible—for example the two versions of the story of "Noah's ark.") Your modern literalist is very different. He demands that the scriptures be simultaneously history in the modern critical sense and in substantial agreement with all branches of modern empirical science, as well as God's saving word, and as such ends up burying the deeper truths of faith under a bushel of accumulated "facts" and other beliefs.

Fundamentalism and Biblical "Inerrancy"

The reason I have focused primarily on this "literalist" aspect of this stage of faith is because it also best uncovers the security-risk tension as well. The basic problem here is not really the supposed conflict between religion and science or even about the *authority* of the Bible and how it is to be interpreted. It is much more a psychological problem at its root. Where children in this stage generally have the trust in their parents and teachers that enables them to separate truth from fiction, it seems that older persons who are caught in this stage seem to have a strong need, above all, for the *security* that authority provides.

Typically, at this stage, faith is seen primarily as *submission* to authority—one "submits" to God and "accepts" Jesus as his or her personal savior—and morality is primarily *conformity* to God's law. There seems to be a striking parallel between Christians caught in this stage and the crisis being faced by the Islamic world. *Islam* means "submission," and a *Muslim* is "one who submits" to the law dictated letter by letter, word for word, to Mohammed in the *Koran*.

For the fundamentalist Muslim, like the fundamentalist Christian, life becomes a holy war against the hostile modern world.

Curiously, such literalistic fundamentalism seems to be a phenomenon of more recent times. One might argue that it is a counterbalance to the insecurity of the modern world with its threat of nuclear disaster and all that. But are these times any more insecure than the plague-ridden past with its almost continual warfare and invasions? I'm not sure that this is the case. But what I do see is that the question of religious authority has become paramount since reformation times.

Most medieval Christians seem to have trusted the authority inherent in the church's tradition even though they may have argued vehemently over the claims of those who would occupy the decisive positions. The reformation destroyed what little semblance of unity there was along those lines and instead attempted to substitute the authority of the Bible alone, to be understood in what the reformers blithely took to be its *obvious*—but not necessarily literal—meaning.

But the "solution" turned out to be part of the problem. What seems obvious to some seems less so to others. Hence, the trend was established toward appealing more and more to what is claimed to be the "literal sense" of scripture, which in turn was invested with the claim of absolute "inerrancy." The Bible, in effect, became a "paper pope."

In addition, theologians and sociologists of religion point out that Christian fundamentalism is almost exclusively an American phenomenon, and that, where it is found in other places in the world, it is almost entirely due to American missionary efforts. This is not surprising, because where else did Protestantism become more unglued from its European theological, cultural, and political foundations but on the American frontier? Indeed, most of the English-speaking American colonials were religious "exiles" from Britain where the Anglican (Episcopal) Church is still the official established church and where for a long time Puritans, Quakers, Catholics and other "dissenters" were only tolerated and on occasion actively persecuted.

So too with many immigrants from other countries; it is no accident that even some forms of the official state religions, like the Lutheranism brought by Scandinavian immigrants, took on a more Protestant "free church" guise on the frontier. Even Catholicism in the early days of the United States showed some of these same free-thinking features. In the days of circuit-riding priests and ministers, home Bible study and lay preaching soon became a feature of American religious life. However, while the level of literacy rose thanks to church schools and community effort to provide children with the "three R's" of "read'n, rite'n, and 'rithmatic," the same cannot be said for the level of biblical understanding. Deprived of sufficient theological education and cut off from the stabilizing tradition of the "mainline" churches of Europe, America grew an exotic variety of religious movements. Even the frontier nicknames conjure up visions of a kind of free-swinging exuberance. Not only did the Society of Friends gain its description as "Quakers" on the American frontier, but Methodists were dubbed "Shouters," Baptists (for obvious reasons) "Dunkers," and, of course, the famous "Shakers" were hardly ever known by any other name. That the various Pentecostalist denominations became known as "holy rollers" and fundamentalists in general are sometimes contemptuously referred to as "Bible thumpers" seems to be part of an old American tradition.

Because of this wealth of names, descriptive or outright derisive, I think it is important that we get a few ideas and terms straight. The title "evangelical," which derives from the Greek word for "gospel," is widely used today to denote a Bible-centered religion and is still used in Europe in place of the term "Protestant" in the names of several churches.

Thus while the adjective "evangelical" generally indicates an emphasis on the Bible, it does not necessarily mean a fundamentalistic or literal approach to reading and interpreting it, even though many calling themselves "evangelicals" today lean in this direction. Furthermore, there is a difference between "fundamentalism" and biblical literalism. "Fundamentalism" as originally conceived meant an emphasis on a few basic truths derived from the New Testament to serve as a program for religious revivalism early in this century. These basic doctrines were seen to be five in number: (1) the inspiration and inerrancy of the Bible, (2) the divinity of Jesus Christ, (3) the atonement accomplished by his death, (4) his actual resurrection, and (5) the future coming of Christ. These are the "fundamentals" that were deemed necessary by these evangelists for salvation.

While most traditional Christians would agree to the centrality of these truths, two of them in particular set the tone that associates "fundamentalism" with the literal interpretation of the Bible. One is the claim of "inerrancy" for the scriptures. Few of the major "mainline" churches insist on this literal kind of interpretation, and instead settle for a belief that the scriptures are an inspired guide to religious truth, but do not hold to the idea that they must be scientifically or even historically accurate on all counts. Where there has been a movement in the direction of claimed "inerrancy," some of the major churches have suffered splits—as that which rent the Missouri Synod Lutherans a few years back.

The other "fundamentalist" emphasis that has caused much dissent is that on the "return of Jesus." Mainline Christianity has tended in recent times to take this belief in the "second coming" in less imminent and sometimes more figurative terms. Fundamentalists, on the other hand, tend to emphasize the closeness of the end-time or the end of the world and the general judgment that will follow. This is obviously a very conversion- and revival-oriented emphasis, and, paradoxically enough, has often depended on a more or less figurative or even symbolic reinterpretation of the apocalyptic visions of the book of Revelation. Certainly, Garner Ted Armstrong's prophecies are not based on strictly literal interpretations. On the contrary, he shows great talent in interpretative innovation. Yet the lure of literalism remains.

To take things further, the mixture of apocalyptic fundamentalism with rigidly "literal" interpretation of the Bible reaches its zenith with the Jehovah's Witnesses. Despite the fact that they attempt to be the most literalist of all fundamentalists, they are not consistently so—a good example being their name for God which is based on a misreading of the Hebrew text ("Jehovah" for "*Yahweh*"). To accomplish this as such, they have tried to disassociate themselves from all traditional Christian doctrinal formulations. Hence, the Witnesses repudiate the doctrine of the Trinity (they don't find that word in the Bible), and while for them Jesus is "divine," he is not God. Nor do they accept the Holy Spirit as anything but divine power—but here they refuse to take the "he" (referring to the Holy Spirit) passages in the gospel of John literally, but only as a mere personification.

The only tradition the Witnesses don't seem to question is that which is rather illogically common to all fundamentalists—the list of books composing the Bible. As is the case with all "inerrantists" they seem to assume that the scriptures came floating down from heaven fully bound with a divinely dictated table of contents. I exaggerate, no doubt, but it is noteworthy how often this obvious gap in reasoning and the ignoring of the history of the biblical canon (the first official Christian lists date from the middle of the fourth century) are all but ignored in fundamentalist circles. To raise the question of how the Bible actually came to us, much less who decided what books belong and which don't, obviously raises too many unsettling questions, especially

when one seeks absolute certainty about one's own rightness
before God and man.

All this is not to criticize the sincerity of fundamentalist
and/or literalist Christians. These churches often elicit a degree of commitment from their members that other Christians would do well to emulate, except for one thing. The
risk that these people undergo in their commitment is too
narrow, too selective. They are willing to risk the scorn of
"unbelievers" (all who don't agree with them) but they are
unwilling to tolerate much less any interior risk, the ambi-
guities of or the real tensions of faith within themselves.
Instead they demand rock-solid certainty at all cost. That
such absolute certainty and security is impossible in this life
should be obvious. If nothing else, this should be clear from
the continual breakups and schisms among these churches
and sects, yet something in their makeup, in their religious
psyche, demands this illusory security at whatever the cost.

You may say: Why bother worrying about these people,
as long as they seem more or less happy in their fancied
certainty? The problem, as I see it, is that they play up directly to the insecurity of so many believers with exactly the
wrong motive based on a defective understanding of faith.
While beckoning to the hesitant to take a "leap" of faith, the
faith they promise is more of a narrowing than a broadening
of vision. What should release us to live more fully too often
ends up as a straitjacket of sorts. Rather than the Christian
freedom from the "law" as proclaimed by St. Paul, we end
up with a new kind of legalism and constraint.

Yet there is more. I suppose it is cruel for me to say so,
but what disturbs me about them is that they, in their claim
to represent pure Christianity, tend to cause all Christians to
be tarred with the same brush—something that I consider to
be most unfortunate, particularly when it comes to the task
of strengthening the ethical foundations of society, a task in
which every committed Christian, as well as every sincere
citizen, should be engaged. Let me explain.

Faith and Morality

When we look at the child in the "intuitive" stage of faith, we find that morality at this level is really more a question of mere "behavior." We do not, or at least should not, hold the child below the age of reason as having true moral responsibility, or fully deserving of merit or guilt. What we do is really try to shape their habits of conduct in a way that will lead them toward moral and ethical goodness in the future. We do this mostly through techniques that modern psychologists call "behavior modification," that is, through employing rewards and punishments. All this is fine and appropriate, providing it is done wisely, with consistency, and with sensitivity. But wisdom dictates that we do not mistake the results with morality. Morality at this level is more in the parents and the teachers than in the child.

However, once a child really begins to exercise reasoning powers we can begin to speak of the child's morality as such. Behavior at this stage continues to have its foundation in persons such as parents, but because it is a behavior that now has truly moral content, the child is naturally going to look for the real moral content in the conduct of the parent. So increasingly parents and other authority figures have to be themselves inspiring of trust. Yet it is only natural in this stage that this trust tends to extend no farther than to the larger "family" community—those of similar class, ethnic, or religious background. So it tends to be a morality that is rather restricted in its scope.

In addition, in its logic, this literal stage morality tends toward "instrumental hedonism"—a more sophisticated, as well as manipulative, form of reward and punishment ethic. Things are seen to be wrong not just because you might get punished, but even more because this or that *authority* said so. But why the authority said so is not very clear. And although the *security* of having this commanding authority now becomes the principal factor, the promise of God's ability to reward (often lavishly) leads all too easily to manipulation and corruption—the recent scandals in TV evangelism being a striking instance in point.

What I have just described is, of course, a normal stage of faith or level of religious comprehension which is appealing in its simplicity, even if its ethical dimensions remain narrow. Unfortunately, at this stage, children's moral vision may be limited more from the example they get from their elders than by any inability to put themselves in the shoes of others—what is called "simple perspective-taking." So if their elders, in turn, have failed to pass beyond a merely literalistic understanding of morality and pass this attitude on to their children by the way they command—as in "Do this and do that . . . don't ask me questions; just do it!"—the result will be to gradually form a society of non-thinking conformists, or, in reaction, just its mirror opposite, non-thinking rebels.

I draw attention particularly to this last point because it appears that a large proportion of the American population if not the majority—but a larger proportion than just those under age thirteen—operates on this pre-ethical level. There is a widespread confusion, especially among the less religious, between what is legal and what is moral, along with a corresponding tendency to think of what you can get away with as being quasi-legal. Either that, or, if a person is more explicitly religious in outlook, moral standards are viewed "nominalistically," which is to say that things are judged either right or wrong simply because "God says so." There is little or no concept of a "natural law" or a divine *Logos* or inherent reason permeating creation.

The result can be seen when it comes to weighty public issues like abortion. On one side we seem to have a supposed "Moral Majority" who want the law to command absolute conformity to what they see as "God's law" against "murder." On the other hand you've got radical "Pro-Choice" people who are rebelling against what they see as a "patriarchal," male-God dominated society by insisting on "control over their own bodies." The real question, as to whether there is really human life at stake, is totally begged by the first group and generally avoided by the latter. Add to this mixture a fair number of "liberal" politicians—among whom are quite a few Catholics—who think they can avoid antagonizing the public by saying: "Personally I'm against it [abortion], but I don't think anyone should foist one's own religious beliefs on the rest of the public, particularly in a pluralistic society such as ours." Now I'm inclined to agree with them, especially the part about dealing with a pluralistic society. I do not think you can really legislate morality as such. But I think abusive behavior can be legislated against (just as we do against child-beating) and that the question of abortion has to be approached first of all from the viewpoint of the natural rights of *all* the parties involved.

In turn, such problems require a more subtle grasp of the relationship between revelation and reason, between the Bible and science, between *morality* as understood as a religious code of conduct binding the believer, and *ethics* as a carefully reasoned philosophy of guiding human society for its own best interests. But for those immersed in the literal stage of faith, such an approach is difficult if not impossible.

In a similar vein, we often hear it said that the United States of America was intended to be a "Christian nation," and that what has been called "Christian reconstructionism"—which is not a church or an organization as such, but a "movement" of fundamentalist-minded believers—must work actively to return American law to biblical norms. But this movement is based on a misreading of U.S. history, ignoring the fact that a good number of our "founding fathers" thought of themselves not as traditional Christians, but as free-thinking "deists," while the rest, many of whom belonged to various "established" churches in the individual colonies, were determined that no official state church be imposed on the United States as a whole. The first amendment to the constitution was expressly designed to forestall any move in that direction. Granted that at the time most Americans were Christians of one sort or another—along with a sprinkling of Jews. Whether they actually foresaw the possibility that Muslims, Hindus, Buddhists and many others would flock to America a century or so later is debatable. But it is obvious that only a more broadly reasoned approach to ethics founded on a philosophy of basic human rights—not to be confused with what has been called a "civil religion"—can even begin to deal with such human diversity.

Conclusion

In a way, societies reproduce the stages of individual human growth. We Americans were often described as an "adolescent" nation. This may still be largely true. But if so, then our long childhood as offspring colonies of a parent European civilization had a certain "mythic" quality about it—take for example our national myth of the first Thanksgiving Day in Plymouth, Massachusetts Colony. The bleak reality can hardly be accurately pictured by the post office muralists, and while something may have been offered them, it is unlikely that the Indians were invited to table. But we need the inspiration the myth provides, providing we in turn don't take it too literally. So we have to see *through* myth lest the literal reading end up missing the whole point. Our reinterpretation of that myth may be still rather adolescent in its bravado—masking a self-doubt still but half-admitted. Yet even such adolescence is but a stage on the way to adulthood. A return to our sectarian childhood is not the way to recapture the vision of America.

So too with the progression of faith in our lives. A return to religious childhood is not the responsible way to go. The myths that sustained it may well retain their intrinsic value, but only if they are "broken open" so as to reveal their inner meanings. The problem with the literal faith stage is that while it may be an easy way to believe, it is seriously lacking when it comes to faith in the full sense of the word. It is a way that not only fails to come to grips with the intellectual challenges of adulthood, but fails to effectively contribute to the ethical qualities that responsible adulthood demands. In its simplistic appeal to "biblical morality"—usually poorly understood—it is counter-productive of any advance toward a mature and ethically responsible society as well. Literal faith is to be expected and even valued in children. But in adults, particularly in those who had once passed beyond it, a literal faith too often represents the evasion of the greater risk that genuine faith demands.

Questions for Reflection and Discussion

1. Who were your childhood heroes or heroines and what religious or moral values did they typify?
2. Describe your childhood social and economic world. Did you feel like an "insider" or an "outsider" in school and society?
3. When did you first begin to make a distinction between biblical stories, historical facts, and universal truth?
4. In your opinion, to what extent do you think biblical or Christian morality should be the standard of public ethics? Why or why not?

5. Conventional Faith

> Some make the world believe that they believe
> what they do not believe. Others, in greater num-
> ber, make themselves believe it, being unable to
> penetrate what it means to believe.
>
> Montaigne

What the great sixteenth century French philosopher
Montaigne was criticizing fits, to a large extent, what is
called by Fowler "synthetic-conventional faith." It is not
called "synthetic" to indicate that it is phony or hypocritical
—although the first type described by Montaigne is so. Nor
is it synthetic in the sense of being artificial, but in that it is
generally reached after something of a personal "synthesis"
or coming together of diverse elements.

But this stage is also "conventional" in the sense that it
is much the same combination of beliefs, attitudes and customs held by one's parents and friends. And because this
stage of faith tends very much to be the level on which many
persons remain, often for the rest of their lives, I will more
often use the second half of Fowler's designation and simply
refer to it as "conventional faith." I do this even though I'm
convinced that in modern society more and more people are
struggling to move beyond this stage, and that probably
most people who read this book have already gone beyond it
in many aspects of their religious life. But unless we try to
understand this stage very thoroughly, we will easily overlook how many elements of it remain, even in those who
have passed a stage or two beyond.

In some societies, like that of the American "Bible
Belt," the conventional level of religious faith may be very
well "literal" in the sense that we discussed "fundamentalism" in the last chapter. On the other hand, in that same

area, the "conventional" level of faith-practice may involve a higher proportion of persons who are more personally committed than is usual—something that we may consider more than conventional by our standards, and that we may well envy or attempt to emulate.

Thus we should not overlook the fact that what is conventional for one society may not be very conventional at all for another. But on the whole the kind of picture given to us by Montaigne still holds true, despite three great revolutions—and here I'm not just referring to the American, French and Russian revolutions, all of which repudiated "state religions," but also of the three great upheavals in human thought and attitudes: the scientific, industrial, and psychological revolutions, each of which was supposed, at its time, to lead to the obsolescence of religious faith. They affected it to be sure, but not nearly as radically as predicted. For the most part, for better or for worse, "conventional faith" remains secure.

Our tasks in the examination of conventional faith will be four: *first*, to take a good look at the characteristics of this stage as they develop in the adolescent; *second*, to examine these same traits as they become, as they so often do, embedded in the general culture; *third*, to look into the causes of why this stage so often seems to persist and interfere with further spiritual growth; finally we'll take a look at the phenomenon of "Catholic traditionalism" as our main example of an attempt to preserve this level of faith.

Adolescence and Conventional Faith

Beginning in the early teen years, the thinking process takes on a more explicitly logical form. The young person, testing various role models, is able to project his or her thought into the roles of others. Human relationships, particularly in the ethical sense, begin to be thought of in terms of mutual responsibility and concord or "getting along with each other." Our perspective also opens out to take in a wider world, at least in symbolic ways. But at the same time, this expanded horizon is necessarily constricted by the still-limited life-experience.

For this reason the "synthesis" in this stage remains a rather tentative one. The components of this synthesis are more or less a combination of family beliefs, influences from school, the surrounding community, and especially from friends. Because the young person is still in the throes of self-discovery, the process at this stage is not so much a matter of balancing one's own inclinations against the lures of the surrounding world as it is using the influences or models presented by the outside world as a means of testing out various roles in the effort to arrive at some provisional idea of oneself. So the result of this "coming together" of various influences, models, roles, etc. is that the young person's faith is very much dependent on participation in various groups—which is why Richard J. Sweeney calls this stage "group faith."

It should be particularly noted that there can be, at the beginning of this stage, a deep religious awakening, but one that is at the same time apt to be greatly confused and interwoven with the search for role identity and the stabilization of emerging sexuality. It is a time of great uncertainty and challenge. The problems involved in confronting and overcoming this uncertainty are equally complex. The central issue is that of emerging *individuality* and to that extent anticipates something of the next stage. But this entails the whole problem of one's relationship to the group (or groups): family, peers, economic and social class, church, even nationality.

It seems that young people, in their efforts to become their own persons, especially need other persons to act as role models, mentors, or even heroes. In a world that increasingly lacks these—would-be candidates, especially in public life, are quickly destroyed by the exposure of the media—the role of the group or class or even "gang" becomes even more exaggerated. The only individuals that seem to stand out these days, at least for long, are such anti-heroes and heroines as the current rock stars. (The late John Lennon's outrageous boast that the Beatles were more famous than Jesus Christ was not without foundation.)

Accordingly, the question of *moral authority,* in particular, takes on new and very serious dimensions. For a young person, the "locus" of authority is no longer so directly connected with this or that authority figure—indeed, there may be a real reaction against all parental or parent-like authority. Instead it more and more becomes focused on the opinion or the conventions of the surrounding society. If you have any doubt about this, just try enforcing an eleven p.m. curfew on your teenager when his or her friends are allowed to stay out to midnight or even to one in the morning. Obviously, even when they are not allowed to prevail, peer pressures are of extreme importance.

At the same time, more directly in terms of faith convictions, the emotional force of *symbols,* which now take on a multidimensional quality, becomes greatly increased. At this stage persons seem less worried about "literal" meanings than before, and while it may sometimes appear that this is for no other reason than that their friends don't seem to be having any such problems, they see no reason why they should worry about such matters. But, at the same time, there may be an opening up to a deeper appreciation for symbolic language, even when it isn't recognized explicitly as such. Under the facade of a kind of blithe cynicism, there actually may be a budding idealism—in fact, the overlay of the tough exterior is usually an instinctual defense of the more vulnerable core.

To understand this phenomenon more thoroughly in its normal development, I turn for help from a somewhat older source, Pierre Babin's *The Crisis of Faith: The Religious Psychology of Adolescence.* This study by the French religious educator (first published as *Les jeunes et la foi* in 1960) has become something of a classic. Despite the passage of the years, much of what it has to say appears to apply very much to American youth. Babin, even more than Fowler, will be our guide in understanding the particularly adolescent elements of the dynamism at work through this stage and even more during the next, even though we will go back to Fowler to assess what it means for faith to become stuck on either of these levels.

At its earliest stage or, better, sub-stage (for as we shall see, Babin distinguishes three phases to adolescence), the reserve ego-strength of the young person is usually not equal to the individuality he or she craves. Hence peer-conformity is generally the outcome. Just how far this conformity takes one toward rebelling against the past depends to a large extent on the same peers on the one hand, and home environment on the other. As any youth counselor knows, the various mixes of influences, and the complications they present, seem endless. But on this level, within this sub-stage, what *security* is available is purchased almost entirely at the *risk* or price of *conformity* of one sort or another. This can be either through conformity to peers which offers a kind of pseudo self-identity or else through a caving in to the demands of one's parents—often with a feeling of loss of self-identity.

During adolescence proper (Babin's second phase) the same factors as the above may still be present, but a certain stabilization, or even truce, between the warring elements occurs. Then the risk becomes one of having achieved peace through some compromise that undermines the basic integrity of the person. In this case security has been achieved by the sacrifice of authenticity. It is not for nothing that young people today criticize so many of the older generation for being what appears to be to them "inauthentic" or "phony" —they fear this in themselves above all! But as we shall see in the next chapter, these early and middle phases of adolescence are really only a threshold to the real challenge of (to use Fowler's words) "becoming an adult, becoming a Christian" and none of this can be accomplished without undergoing, in some sense, a "crisis of faith."

The adolescent believer is a very difficult subject to accurately describe and is very much a person still in the process of becoming himself or herself. No wonder there seems to be great inconsistency. Yet despite the sketchiness of this description of adolescent faith, the fact that these same characteristics are shared by a large number of American adults should give us pause to think. The fact that most TV entertainment is purposely geared to the mentality—despite its supposed "adult" subject matter—of the early teens may disgust us. And when sloganeering replaces any attempt to engage in reasoned persuasion, as we have seen in recent election campaigns, we should be alarmed, but not entirely surprised. Little real thinking is involved in conventional attitudes. Much the same is true for conventional faith.

Society and Security

In some ways, what we call "conventional faith" represents a synthesis of many "faiths," that is, it represents a combination of beliefs and ideologies belonging to one or another of the many groups to which we belong, all at the same time. This is particularly true of the combination of religious identity and the ideals of society. Just the very day that I began a revision of this chapter, I heard a sample of this on the radio in the campaign song of a candidate for the U.S. presidency. The candidate, a former TV evangelist of wide following, was being touted as standing, above all, "for God and country"—a catchy and appealing phrase, which, among other things, was also the name of a coveted award for outstanding Boy Scouts.

Nothing wrong in this, we might say. But have we pondered the implications of too close an association between these two values of religion and patriotism? Should not all the bloody wars fought in the name of religion, even when religion was being only used as a mask for racial, ethnic, or even just economic privilege, make us suspicious of such a close association between the two? Abraham Lincoln, when asked if he thought that God was on *our* (the Union) side, responded that we should rather be asking ourselves whether or not we are on *God's* side. Too often the ready assumption of conventional faith is that we are automatically in the right.

What kind of faith then is "conventional" or typical of our society? I think we need only listen to our politicians when they are running for office to get a pretty good idea of what Fowler means. We hear frequent references to the American heritage and its values, particularly its respect for "freedom," "integrity," "individual responsibility" and "honest work," and often, in the same breath, to the "Judeo-Christian" tradition. Recently we have seen examples of political leaders or government agencies and policy setting departments making theological pronouncements as to what is the meaning of the scriptures when it comes to setting economic policies, or, on the contrary, bitter criticism of the churches when they suggest that the present order of our society violates some of the basic standards of social justice.

All this is symptomatic of what sociologists often call "civil religion"—a confusion of patriotism, religious institutionalism, and the status quo. But what inspires these confusions between patriotism and religious faith? No doubt our security needs have a lot to do with it. To know that "God is on our side," or even to be sure that we are on God's side, has a tremendous potential for reassuring ourselves in a hostile world. This is readily understandable—but is it defensible?

One of the hallmarks of conventional thinking is its insularity. It is more than just a curious fact that when one goes back far enough into the history of human language, almost inevitably a people's name for themselves turns out to simply be "the people" as if other peoples were not quite human beings. Typically too, as the late anthropologist Margaret Meade pointed out, you can almost infallibly measure the degree of ethical advancement of a civilization in terms of the extent that it applies the commandment or idea "thou shall not kill" to people other than those of one's own tribe or race. The record of the world's great cultures, despite Toynbee's contention that all the great civilizations had their beginning in religious roots, has not been inspiring in this regard. Instead of helping to extend the understanding of the sacredness of life as applying to other people as well as one's own, too often the politically tainted theologies of conventional faith have been used to justify the killing of those of other religious beliefs.

Another sign of the arresting of faith at the conventional level is its emphasis on the "law and order" concept of morality. We have already seen, when we discussed "biblical morality" how literal faith tends toward a very superficial grasp of ethical principles. For the literal-minded, the essence of something being a "law" is simply that God has "ordered" or commanded it to be so. There is little grasp of *why* or *how* such a command fits into the greater scheme or order of things. But for the conventional "law and order" mentality, the reasoning is only slightly more advanced and in one aspect even slightly retrogressive. Unlike those of literal faith, they now begin to see how this or that command contributes to the right order of things in the world, but on the other hand they seem to have lost the sense of the divine freedom or prodigality of grace.

Why is this so? It is probably because such an idea of God's freedom to forgive threatens our individualistic concept of justice. Our conventional morality of checks and balances is as neatly ordered as Newton's mechanical universe, which works fine enough within the context of society composed neatly along the same lines. The only trouble is that, like the expanding universe revealed by Einstein and modern science, our world and human society is immensely more complicated than that. Yet conventional wisdom continues to insist on an ethical system that, although refined and modified down through the course of ages, had its roots in the stone age. "To each his due" or "to every man according to the value of his work" seems to be the watchword of this conventional morality, because if we were to allow that material wealth, like the sunshine and the rain, might be distributed to "sinner and the just" alike, then we might have to admit that our fortunes could be just as insecure as the weather. In the eyes of conventional faith, the gospel injunctions not to worry about our future needs are, of course, not to be taken too seriously—nor, would it seem, contemporary church teachings about a Christian "preferential option for the poor."

Finally, the crucial moral test which shows the inadequacy of conventional faith is not so much in the matter of ideas of justice, but in the scope and practice of Christian *love*. The so-called "golden rule" is typically touted by conventional faith as the epitome of Christian morality when in fact one form or another of it is found in almost all the world's religions and ethical systems—for example, the Confucian dictum "Do not do to others what you would not have them do to you." To "love one's neighbor as oneself" is no big step forward in the evolution of morality, unless one can extend, as Jesus did, the concept of "neighbor" to include *all* human beings, particularly those who are most unfortunate. Even more beyond the scope of this limited sense of justice is to "love your enemies, and to do good to those who persecute you." It is this distinctively Christ-like love—"By this all will know you, that you love one another as I have loved you" (Jn 13:35)—that distinguishes a committed Christian faith from conventional religiosity, that separates mature or maturing faith from merely adolescent ideals.

Oddly enough, in this last aspect conventional faith often fails to measure up even to the faith and generosity found in many adolescents. Why is this so? The difference is, I believe, in the fact that during the adolescent phase, although faith may be very "conventional" in style, being as it is, a synthesis of the many values and standards to which the young person is exposed, it is nevertheless part of an ongoing process in which everything is being continuously sorted out and re-thought and which—as we shall see—must sooner or later confront one crisis after another. There is little time or oppor-tunity to become complacent in one's faith. Faith at this growing stage of life is seen as part of the armament one will need to fight the battles to come. The situation is quite differ-ent for the supposedly "mature" adult.

Conscientious Conformism

If the quotation from Montaigne, at the beginning of this chapter, seemed harsh, the judgment of the great turn-of-the-century Russian novelist and religious and social thinker, Leon Tolstoy, seems even more critical.

> ... the vast majority, poor, uneducated, but for the most part truly sincere, remain under the hypno-tism of the Church, and therefore think they believe and have faith. But this is not *really* faith. . . . (Tol-stoy, *What Is Religion?*—emphasis mine)

Granted that conditions in twentieth century America are vastly different from those in nineteenth century Russia, why does the average American, or the average person of any nationality, remain in this typical class of believers and proceed no farther? Or, to ask this question in another way, why do Montaigne's and Tolstoy's indictments of popular religiosity still strike a responsive and uncomfortable chord? One might think that, once a state-supported church or official religion was done away with, people would be forced to decide for themselves in matters of faith. In some ways this is true, but what inevitably happens is that even without official state sanction, family and ethnic or cultural tradition tends to win over all. So once the adolescent process of sorting out just where one belongs is more or less complete, it seems that, short of a major upheaval of some sort, this synthesis, no matter how many contradictions or compromises it may contain, is apt to remain one's chosen faith—if one can speak of "choice" in this sense.

We should particularly focus on Tolstoy's harsh words about the role of the churches in this matter. Granted that Tolstoy was an "anarchist" who believed that governments were only a conspiracy of the rich to enslave the poor, and that the official church—in this case, the Russian Orthodox Church—was only a willing co-conspirator in this plot, still Tolstoy's words, no matter how exaggerated, bear some truth, especially when the authority and prestige of religion are used to sanction the *status quo,* as was the case in imperial Russia, by means of crowning the tsar, blessing his wars, and assuring the downtrodden peasants that heaven would be their reward for being obedient serfs. Marx and Lenin rightly called such use of religion "the opiate of the people." But how about less extreme cases, particularly in the more democratic and pluralistic west?

Looking back over the policies of the Christian churches in our culture, there can be no doubt that what organized religion has generally expected from its members has been, to a large extent, this synthetic or conventional faith. The emphasis on the education of the young almost had to be, by design, aimed at this level of development. Once inculturated into this level, young men and women, most of whom would receive no further education of any sort, could be expected to fit nicely into the communities of family, civil society, and church. Further growth in commitment and in "holiness," of course, was encouraged. But other aspects of faith development were generally discouraged, precisely because they were deemed to be "dangerous to one's faith."

Despite the obvious advantages it affords, particularly from the institutional viewpoint, the price paid by such a policy has been enormous. Speaking as a Roman Catholic who grew up before the Second Vatican Council, I think that I, with so many others of my generation, can see now how completely unprepared the bulk of American Catholics were for the changes brought about by the council. I say this not so much about the liturgical changes (mass in the vernacular, communion in the hand, etc.) but about the general atmosphere of freedom and especially its accompanying responsibilities. If so many Catholics, including some of the clergy and professional "religious," began to carry on like a group of adolescents, it was probably because they had never experienced what it was like to be treated as an adult.

Has the situation changed in recent years? Although I'm convinced that the statistics have probably changed, I'm sure that "synthetic-conventional" faith remains predominant. This is not just because what is synthetic and conventional is, by definition, an amalgam of what other people generally hold. If, since the enlightenment, the reformation, the scientific revolution, and the like, the conventional level of faith has shifted from "mythic-literal" to a more "synthetic" mode of understanding, this does not necessarily mean that the amount of personal commitment has necessarily increased along with this shift. One can be just as much one of the "sheep" by following not so much the leader as just following the rest of the flock.

Similarly, if since Vatican II most American Catholics now seem more open to ecumenical sharing, less dependent on authority figures, less threatened by secular society, none of this necessarily translates into greater commitment. The flock on a whole, with some notable exceptions, has moved in these directions. On the other hand, because this general drift has seemed to bring with it a lessening of rigid adherence to church directives, one must be careful about not taking the statistics from studies limited to those who are still active Catholics. I would suspect that an in-depth study (like those done through Fowler's interviews) would show a higher degree of personal commitment among regular weekly church-going Catholics today than thirty years ago. But if one were to poll *all* those who still call themselves "Catholic" to some degree or another, I suspect the degree of commitment might be considerably less, even less than that of thirty years prior.

I will not attempt to make similar guesses regarding members of other Christian denominations. Even if I did, I suspect that the results would vary greatly depending on whether a person identified with the so-called "main-line" churches (here one would expect to find results similar to Catholics taken across the board) or with a more "evangelical" or even "fundamentalist" group—where I would expect more commitment, but a bit less development in other aspects. However, if one simply looks at the American public in general, the prognosis for a general breakthrough in faith development is not promising. In our society of instant communication, it seems even the "born-again Christian" movement toward a more personal faith easily degenerates into a fad.

"Conventional" faith, then, remains the slipperiest of the faith stages, to a large extent because of its "synthetic" characteristics; it tends toward an amalgam, a blend of one's own personal tendencies and quirks with that of the society in which one lives. So a great amount of compromise is involved.

For this reason Daniel A. Helminiak borrows the term "conscientious conformism" from Jane Loevinger's 1977 study on *Ego Development* to describe this latter part of the conventional faith stage, particularly when it becomes constant in a person's life. Where early adolescence tends, in its insecurity, simply toward mere, unthinking conformism, later adolescence moves on into a conscientious or more personally reasoned or rationalized conformism. Fowler, in fact, admits that there is a kind of "stage three (or four) and a half" that more exactly describes "synthetic-conventional" faith, especially when it becomes the fixed state in an otherwise adult believer.

If one were to describe this "stage and a half," it would look something like a recipe for a lemon meringue pie: whip together equal parts of family tradition, childhood religious education and civil religion. Add one tablespoon of personal ambitions and pour the mixture into the pre-shaped crust of peer pressures. Top with a layer of pious practices and sprinkle with some of the latest ideas from Vatican II and some more recent "in" things, and half-bake until more or less fixed enough to resist upsetting if tipped!

If the above recipe seems a bit silly or even harsh, I suggest we take a good look at ourselves. How did we arrive at where we are when it comes to our faith? Too often we seemed only to take what appeared to be the bottom line demands of our faith, adjusted the limits a little here and there to fit our own personal ambitions, added some extras to please God and other onlookers, and probably ended up thinking that we were being reasonably "religious"—not fanatic, mind you, but respectably "devout." It is sad that this accommodation can still turn out to be the average level of commitment in even a "renewed" post-Vatican II church; but how else can we explain the phenomenon where hundreds of thousands can turn out to see the pope make a personal appearance, but totally ignore his teachings on justice and peace, much less *risk* putting them into practice?

Catholic Traditionalism

If the "conscientious conformism" of the conventional post-Vatican II Catholic can be described as something like the above, how can we describe the would-be pre-Vatican II

Catholic "traditionalist"? How can we explain a church where, having finally confronted the challenges of the modern age, and having decided to meet them head-on, a significant minority now decides that things have gone too far in the direction of modernization, and now, if they had their way, would retreat to the "certainties" of the past, to a "fortress-Catholicism" that idolizes the "Christendom" of the high middle ages, or appeals to the "irreformable" doctrines of Vatican I and Trent as being the norm and ideal of Catholic understanding and culture?

We have already seen, in the last chapter, how literal faith, while it often naturally remains strong among people who have a little educational background, very often has its greatest appeal to those who have found their security threatened in some way or who have become alienated from society in general. In some ways literalistic fundamentalism is a throwback made up of a rejection of merely conventional religiosity and, at the same time (as we shall see), a step that reassures many in the throes of coming to a truly personal faith.

Although the reaction of some Catholics to the changes introduced by Vatican II shows many of these same traits, including widespread ignorance of what the council actually said—indeed some polls at the time showed that many lesser educated Catholics were not even aware that Vatican II was taking place—I suspect that many self-styled Catholic "conservatives" are really fleeing the risks of acquiring a personal faith, rather than consciously undertaking the task of forging out a new synthesis and renewing their commitment on this basis.

Of course, some people of this mind may see such a retrenchment—which they see simply as a "return" or "restoration"—as a risk that must be taken in order that Catholicism may get its house back in order. But I can't avoid thinking that such a tactic is really an attempt to buy back the *security* that these people feel that their religion no longer provides. The loss of the sense of security (or what was thought to be the security) of the old ways may be, in some way, regrettable, but this does not justify this impossible effort to turn back the clock.

Oddly enough, some of the changes that have been most objected to were, in effect, an effort to recover some of the most ancient values and authentic ways of Catholic worship and tradition. For example, what was most "traditional" about the use of Latin? Was it that it had become a "dead language" which sounded familiar but which very few understood, or was it instead that it had once been the vernacular which was adopted only after Greek ceased to be the most widely understood language in the Roman Church? In other words, the authentic principle that stands behind the ancient tradition is to use the vernacular of the people. It was all but inevitable that a misunderstood "traditionalism" which had attempted to arrest the natural *evolution* of belief and practice had to give way to what seemed a veritable *revolution* in Vatican II in order to effectively address the needs of the times. True, "opening the windows" of the church, as Pope John XXIII put it, involved the risk of polluted air entering, even while the stale air had become increasingly unbreathable within. But—to change the image somewhat—the situation had become like a pressure cooker with a stuck valve. If the internal pressure for reform, which had been largely frustrated since the counter-reformation four centuries earlier, had not been given vent, it is more likely that the whole pot would have blown up. That there has been a lot of steam and some boiling over instead was only to be expected.

Either way, these efforts are not without risk, for life cannot be effectively lived in the past, whether it be ancient times or merely the immediate past. A living faith, like life itself, must be a growing thing—it cannot be effectively preserved under glass or pickled in formaldehyde. The attempt to arrest growth at any particular stage, or to fix its expression in the customs and trappings of any one era, does not result in simply a suspension of growth but more often in death and decay. Too often what were only temporary weaknesses sooner or later become permanent disabilities. Or as we see in the case of both biblical fundamentalism and Catholic traditionalism, there may even be a reversion to an earlier, less developed and less adequate stage.

As David Viscott's list of cautions, at the end of his book *Risking,* indicates, not every risk is a wise one. And a risk that is motivated primarily by a nostalgia for the past is a folly of the highest order, for the past, as such, no longer exists. Faith may indeed call us back to the fidelity of the past, but it can only do so in the context of the present and with a vision of the future. Conventional faith fails, particularly when it takes on the form of "traditionalism," not in its sincerity, and especially not in its sense of solidarity with the past. Instead, it fails precisely as a lack of *faith* to the extent that it tends to retreat to these relics of past security and to seek refuge in them.

Conclusion

In sum, we must admit that despite all its strengths and especially its sense of solidarity, conventional faith for the most part not only is a rather immature faith, but in some ways is not real faith at all. There is a certain confidence, to be sure, born of convictions to which real commitment has been given, yet, as is so obvious when held up in comparison to the demands of the gospel, something essential is missing. What is it?

To answer this, we will be compelled not only to look beyond, but also to look deeply within and to confront ourselves with some very searching and perhaps uncomfortable questions, not just about the contents of our faith, but even more about our motives. Truly committed belief or genuine faith may not be really possible until some "crisis of faith" has been undergone.

What we have called "conventional faith" should really be seen as no more than what is a way-stop encountered in the midst of adolescence. Yet, it continues to be the stage lived by many, if not the majority of, "believers"—even in modern America. Increasingly, this attempt to freeze faith in the conventional stage becomes more untenable. We are compelled either to move forward or else slip back; otherwise sooner or later something will have to give.

If, according to Frankl, religion is "the *search* for ultimate meaning," then it follows that however much faith—in the sense of confidence—we already have, genuinely living, growing faith cannot give up commitment to the continued search. And while we all crave the security that faith alone can give us, this security is a grace that can only come to us if we are willing to undergo the risk of moving forward in a committed effort to deepen our experience and understanding of God. Where the synthesis in "conventional faith" is entirely natural in the searching adolescent and still-searching young adult, it is too often, for those who have given up the search, a compromise that is something less than genuine faith. It becomes—to put it in existentialist terms—"bad faith" or "bogus faith," a "cheap grace" for which we have paid with very little risk of ourselves. No doubt there is real risk in moving forward, but as has often been pointed out, in many life-threatening situations, the greatest risk is in doing nothing at all. The life of faith can be no exception.

Questions for Reflection and Discussion

1. List, to the extent you can, the various elements or components of the faith that you had as a young person of high school age. Did the various elements harmonize well or not? Give examples.
2. Who were your heroes (or heroines) during your teenage years? Were they the same or different than those of childhood. Why?

3. At what point in your life was your faith first challenged? Did your faith grow or diminish as a result of that challenge? How and why?

4. Can you see any possible conflicts in your own life between love of God and love of your country? If so, how do you think you can resolve them?

5. What did you find most attractive about the "old" (pre-Vatican II) church? What was least attractive? How would you evaluate your present faith stance?

6. (Bonus Problem) You have a sixteen year old daughter who refuses to attend Sunday mass and demands to stay home to listen to Madonna and Michael Jackson records instead. How do you think this should be handled? Or you have a nineteen year old son who refuses to register for Selective Service—what will you say to him? What will you say to the neighbors once they find out?

6. Personal Faith

Faith means battles; if there are no contests, it is
because there are none who desire to contend.

St. Ambrose

This observation was made at the end of the age of martyrs, over fifteen hundred years ago. Those who joined the
church were no longer in much danger of being thrown to
the lions, but the official political recognition of Christianity
had brought an even greater danger to the life of faith. For if
faith is to be anything beyond merely conventional conformity to the prevailing culture, it will demand personal
struggle. When faith ceases to be clearly in opposition to the
world at large, the danger is that any real desire to commit
oneself will be either co-opted by alternative counter-
cultural movements or all but swallowed up by sham religiosity.

This challenge to become fully authentic in one's commitment is the call to achieve what James Fowler calls "in-
dividuative-reflective faith," and what I, along with Richard
Sweeney, call "personal faith." Even though we will take a
more careful look at why Fowler uses the words he does, this
level of faith is most of all, in my estimation, *personal* not
only because it represents one's personal choice, but because it is deeply involved in the process of our becoming an
individual in the sense of being the unified or undivided
person that each of us should be.

Although I would prefer to reserve the term *individua-
tive* to the next stage (the "conjunctive") for reasons that I
will explain in the next chapter, this stage is highly individual not just because it is a product of one's individuality, but
also because it actually contributes to the personal identity
of the maturing person. Just as, on a biological level, "we are

what we eat," so also on the level of our psychological and spiritual being, we tend to become what our convictions and commitment urge us to be. The world-view that we hold to, the meanings that we have for our existence, and the particular role that we assume for ourselves in life: all these are part of the unique individual that each of us is. True, there is apt to be a lot of trial and error in this process, especially when it comes to adjusting the particular limitations that are "givens" in our life to the grander ideals and schemes of meaning. But even here, it is the particular adjustments or even compromises that each individual makes in this process that establish one's personal identity.

Such a process, of course, cannot take place without considerable thought or *reflection*. However, there is not only an increase in the amount of thinking, but even more it is the *quality* of that thought which makes this stage truly "reflective." The person begins to think in more strictly structured logic, often dichotomizing issues in either/or propositions. One's picture of the world takes on more explicit, definitive form, and symbolic patterns of thinking tend to be scorned. As a result, for many who are educated in our modern schools, the beginning of this stage of life is marked by a rejection of belief in religious "myth" in favor of a new belief in "scientific" reasoning.

So, too, moral reasoning undergoes a similar process— indeed, sometimes with all the vehemence of a reflex reaction to the moralisms of earlier stages of religious development. Morality, which tends to emphasize the stress on obedience to divine commands, finds itself challenged to become a more systematically reasoned *ethics*. This process begins particularly when a person becomes more aware of cultural differences in moral thinking and begins to develop a more relativistic point of view. The young person is not so much shocked by people who have abandoned all morality as he or she is puzzled by persons whose sincere ideas of what is right or wrong seem to be very different, yet just as conscientious, as his or her own. The challenge here, is, of course, to see beyond the particulars and to develop a more universal ethic in keeping with a broadened world-view.

Here it should be cautioned, however, that a significant difference should be noted between women and men when it comes to moral reasoning. Researcher Carol Gilligan has faulted the work of Lawrence Kohlberg, who (like his preddecessor Jean Piaget) based his stages of moral reasoning almost exclusively on studies made with boys. Women, according to Gilligan, seem to exhibit a more "relativistic" style of moral reasoning due to their tendency to emphasize personal relationship over abstract principles. In this sense women also are less likely to succumb to the rigid "law and order" mentality that accompanies conventional faith as well as naturally anticipate the perspective-taking flexibility that characterizes a more advanced "conjunctive" faith. (See Carol Gilligan's "Woman's Place in Man's Life Cycle," reprinted from *The Harvard Educational Review,* and further refinements of Kohlberg's theory by John Michael Murphy and Carol Gilligan in Margaret Gorman's *Psychology and Religion: A Reader,* pp. 203–214.) One would expect that due to a more intuitive style of thought, women are less likely to reject symbolic patterns of thinking at this stage as well.

Still, whatever development takes place, whether in young women or young men, is still apt to be biased, not just in favor of their own ideals, but even more by the social class or group that embodies these values. So while inherited authority figures may be viewed with suspicion, there remains a strong need for self-chosen role-models who become new authority figures for the person moving into this stage. In fact, some studies have shown that the more idealistic a person is at this stage the more he or she is susceptible to being attracted to various so-called "cults," particularly those led by a charismatic personality.

One can predict, from all these tensions, that the movement into personal faith is not always a smooth one. If nothing else, it will usually be punctuated by conflicts with persons who are content to remain in the conventional stage and are apt to be threatened by the questioning that the movement into a more mature faith demands. But even without this environmental static, the person struggling to move into this faith level will often experience an inner turmoil caused by the strong tendency to think in terms of over-generalized opposites. Things tend to be either black or white, right or wrong—there seems little room for shades of meaning or degrees of truth. All this tends to produce a crisis situation, a turning point in one's faith life. So crucial is this period for one's further growth that we must examine it more in detail.

Crisis and Conversion

As we saw in the previous chapter, Pierre Babin had already traced back in the 1950s what he believed were the adolescent "stages in the growth of faith" and even suggested that despite the important formative influences of the earlier stages (childhood, pre-adolescence, and pubescent adolescence), it is only beginning in *late adolescence* that anything like a true act of faith is possible. All that has gone before—the essential relationship of the infant toward its parents, the socialization of the child into the life of community and church, the first questionings of pre-adolescence, and even the sometimes passionate religious quest that characterized early and mid-adolescence—is only, as Babin sees it, "a beginning and a call." But all this adds up to something more as well, both a risk and a challenge:

> . . . a *risk;* but . . . also . . . a privileged moment because of the intensity of the search and the questions . . . the religion of childhood which was accepted unquestioningly does not suffice. Man must

come to a *personal* religion, in which he knows himself by his own proper name in the body of Christ (Babin, p. 99—emphasis mine).

Describing the process by which the young person comes to a personal faith, Babin writes of an ". . . evolution that follows a triple rhythm, like waves that overlap; a state of doubt and *deep insecurity;* a state of reflection and intellectual deepening; a state of decision, commitment, emphasizing the direction chosen" (Babin, p. 101—emphasis mine). He then goes on to speak of the young person, at age seventeen, despite the stabilization of biological drives as being "—in certain respects especially—more *insecure,* more distraught than ever. . . . At the same time his *insecurity,* which had until now been affective, becomes more and more intellectual and reflective" (Babin, pp. 102–103—again, emphasis mine).

Babin then reflects a little further on this. The crisis is not specifically intellectual as such; it is only partly so—and less so than it will be later. But it is brought about by a lethal triad of "emotional shock" (often following a failed love affair), "remorse," and "deep affective and intellectual insecurity." Babin sees also that often this affective and intellectual insecurity ". . . frequently takes on symptoms of moral insecurity," and that together, all this leads to a crisis where the young person either gives up the practices of Christian life or else will lead to a decision that opens up to grace. "The necessity of a choice becomes clear: either a greater depth of faith, or lapse from the faith" (Babin, p. 104).

Despite the insistence of this challenge, the choice can be put off. Babin sees this often happening, partly because in our age there is such a range of options that commitment to any one choice becomes increasingly difficult. It is almost as if the almost unlimited range of possibilities at the same time brings with it a paralysis like that afflicting the fabled donkey of Greek philosophy; standing between two piles of hay and equally attracted to both, the beast eventually starved to death. So for many, especially the young:

> Between these two paths of evolution—the one positive, the other negative—there remains a third, an incomplete path. Many young people never make the transition from childish or adolescent attitudes to maturity, whether through dissipation, evasion, cowardice, fear, or general lack of maturity (Babin, p. 115).

So we see from this analysis that this crisis of late adolescence can lead to one of three outcomes. According to Babin there can be a real deepening of faith, or else even an outright refusal of faith. But all too often there can simply be an arrestment, a refusal to move on.

When Babin speaks of "conversion," as he does in the second chapter of his book, he distinguishes three types. The first, "*explicit conversion,*" he describes as

> . . . the act or event in which the young person gives his life a direction and meaning in relation to transcendent values, with a depth of consciousness and decision that put an end to the vacillations of his adolescence and profoundly affect the moral and religious sense of his adult life (See Babin, 1959, p. 60).

The second and third forms of conversion, which Babin terms "*implicit*" and "conversion through the *ratification* of a given situation," are allied to the first, but less directly so. Much here hinges on temperament and circumstances and we will have occasion to reflect on these variant forms later in this chapter. But for now, I think we must focus on *explicit* conversion which not only illustrates the biblical sense of the word "conversion," or *metanoia* (translated literally, the "change of mind" or of manner of thinking) but also because it best emphasizes the kind of commitment that is involved in the passage from conventional to personal faith.

This original biblical meaning of the word is very important for our understanding of this critical stage of faith development. "Conversion" has too often become associated with the idea of changing religions or switching churches. As Fowler points out, such a change can occur along with the movement into this more personally reflective stage of faith—but not necessarily. Quite the contrary, a change of church or religion could be in many cases a strategy for avoiding any deepening of faith (See Fowler, 1979, pp. 281–82).

At the same time, the kind of religious "intensification experiences" (a term borrowed by Fowler from R.M. Moseley) brought about by revivals, retreats, or other such religious exercises often can be the catalyst that helps one move into a more personal faith, but they should not be confused with the actual stage change itself. Likewise, the moral renewal that often takes place along with these experiences also can be a part of a genuine conversion—but such a renewal also can represent only a minor change in attitude within the same faith stage. For example, a person may simply decide it's more in his or her self-interest to tread the "straight and narrow path" than be a "sinner" yet persist in the same kind of selfish thinking that led him or her into the life of sin.

It is important that we understand these distinctions, because without them we will not have a really clear idea of what a truly personal faith demands from us. The result, as we shall see, can be fatal to our spiritual development. As Babin warned, the challenge of personal faith cannot be ignored. True, we can either accept the challenge in its entirety and advance, or flatly reject the summons. But too often, compromise of some sort prevails. But even to understand these, we must first examine the more obvious examples of the underlying psychological patterns that are involved.

Excesses and Regressions in Personal Faith

At first glance, there may seem to be a contradiction in terms involved in grouping excesses in faith along with regressions in faith, but on closer examination we will see that the two occurrences are usually closely related. What often strikes us most negatively about persons who have undergone conversion or even simple "intensification experiences" as described above is their tendency to become fanatic and intolerant of all others who do not agree with them. It is probably safe to say that this trait is more often the cause —or at least the excuse—of others turning away from religious faith than all other reasons combined.

This phenomenon has several causes. One is the sheer overwhelmingness of the conversion experience. A person often does feel really as if he or she had been "born again." True, such feelings may vary widely in intensity and expression depending on temperament and other circumstances, but, generally speaking, we could say that a conversion, especially when combined with an intensification experience, can be not unlike falling in love—one's entire world seems bathed in a whole new light.

Another cause of this tendency is often rooted more directly in the psychological dynamics of youth. Young people, who can often seem unmercifully judgmental toward others, especially toward older people and their institutions, are often really projecting on others their own intolerance toward themselves. This tendency toward self-perfectionism, accompanied by severe criticism of the imperfections of others, is, of course, the flip side of what is otherwise the admirable idealism of youth. Yet this situation is not restricted to youth. Persons, at any age, who undergo a genuine moral conversion are likely to be hard on themselves, and to the extent that this process is unconscious, to that extent they tend to become all the more judgmental toward others.

We are all too familiar with the ex-smoker syndrome, but often the problem goes deeper than just a revulsion for one's former way of life. More like the reformed alcoholic than the ex-smoker who no longer can stand the stench of tobacco, the newly born-again Christian may still be battling strong attractions and temptations to return to his or her old haunts. What may on the surface look like an excess of faith and confidence is often just the opposite—a mask hiding, even from himself or herself, what is really a very insecure faith, or even an outright lack of faith at least as far as confidence is concerned. This is the point where an apparent excess of faith is really the occasion of a *regression* back into some of the most striking features of what are earlier stages of faith.

One of the most common examples of this danger in the movement into personal faith can be seen when religious "conversion" involves an outright reversion to the literal stage, sometimes mixed with the more negative elements of intuitive faith. As we have seen, much of American "born again" Christianity exhibits these traits. Not that these Christians are not sincere, or even that their faith commitment is not a personal one. But this genuinely personal commitment is mixed up with certain security needs that have taken on the literalistic and fundamentalistic approaches to biblical interpretation described in Chapter 4.

We have also seen (in Chapter 5) that something similar often happens with persons in the more outspoken wings of Catholic "traditionalism"—although many who identify with this movement in some way may be simply stuck in the "conventional" stage of faith. Yet there can be no doubt that at least some of these traditionalists, like many of their fundamentalist counterparts, are genuine "converts" in the biblical sense of the word, having undergone a real change in thinking, perhaps involving a moral conversion as well. At the same time, their inner insecurity drives them to fall back to reliance on certain aspects of a less mature stage of faith, most typically the familiar certitudes of what was once a comfortably "conventional" faith, if not occasionally to some of the worst compulsive aspects of the "intuitive" faith of early childhood.

Many of these same traits are seen in the example that I have put off discussing until this moment—the "charismatic renewal." This movement has become popular among many Roman Catholics and members of other major Christian "main-line" denominations, sweeping through these churches, particularly in North America, since the late 1960s. Among Catholics it first appeared just where one would have expected it least—among college students and not a few of their professors. At the time it perhaps could be seen as an antidote to the pseudo-intellectual bent that Catholic religious education had been taking with its cut-and-dried "we've got an answer for everything, even if you didn't ask" approach. Such indoctrination, even dressed up on the college level in the guise of Thomistic theology, left most Catholic students highly informed about the faith, but without any real experience of it.

Soon after, when the same movement spread to the parish, some disturbing new phenomena appeared. One was the almost constant preoccupation with the extraordinary, especially with *glossolalia* or "the gift of tongues," "prophecy," "healings" and other demands for new signs of the miraculous. Coupled with this was a growing division, not only between those "baptized in the Spirit" and those who felt no need for this, but among the charismatics themselves, particularly when it came to questions of leadership. Yet one could honestly expect that such difficulties can afflict, and usually do, any movement, particularly one that was challenging Catholics to move from conventional to a more personal faith—which was exactly what this movement was most effectively doing. As we have seen, such either/or thinking and its attendant polarization are to be expected at this stage.

But something else began to occur that was not to be so readily expected. Some Catholic charismatics, feeling an ecumenical kinship with charismatics of other churches (and sometimes sensing a cold shoulder from their own leadership), began to drift into the more openly "pentecostalist" type denominations or others largely given over to fundamentalist-literalist biblical interpretation. With some, there was even a rejection of what they now deemed to be charismatic emotionalism for a new-found scriptural certitude. Not that a combination of the two tendencies is not often found. For example, both fundamentalists and charismatics occasionally resort to "divining" scriptures—that is, of finding particular answers to personal problems by opening up the Bible at random to find a passage that seems to give a specific answer. In any case, what often happens represents, to a large extent, a type of reversion to "literal" faith, one prompted by a need for *security*—the intellectual security that a charismatic outpouring of pentecostal charisms couldn't fill.

If, in some ways, the results of what seemed a promising movement have been disappointing, it is because what began as both a challenge and a means toward developing a personal faith too often ended up in a retreat into pietistic isolation and biblical literalism. But I do not think this has been due to lack of generosity and the desire of persons to commit themselves. If anything, the failure has been due to an excess of this willingness without solid enough leadership or astute guidance. But even more, the failure is due to a lack of a more balanced and dynamic concept of faith.

In any case, these examples of a more positive desire to grow in faith that have in some fashion gone astray have at least a strong potential for rehabilitation and reorientation upon a more solid path. The spirit is still willing, even if "the flesh"—the form this openness to the life of faith has taken —has taken some strange turns. The same, I think, cannot be said about those whose failure in commitment has to be characterized more as a simple refusal of faith.

The Refusal of Faith

So far we have concentrated on contrasts between as well as combinations of the first and the last of the three possible outcomes of the faith crisis—namely, genuine conversion as contrasted to various compromises or evasions that may cause a regression into certain earlier stages of faith. But there is another possibility according to Babin's view—an outright refusal of faith.

Is it possible to *lose* one's faith? Typically, young persons in churches that attempt to protect their members' faith are often warned against the dangers of this happening. Yet somewhat contradictorily we are sometimes assured that one cannot "lose" the faith—that one can only "throw it away."

How true is this? Recently I saw another variation of this same contention in the question and answer column of a Catholic newspaper where the priest-columnist claimed that "No one has ever left the faith over doctrinal reasons." His explanation of this sweeping generalization seems to have implied that since "the faith" was practically self-evident as "the truth," there are inevitably moral reasons behind anyone's falling away from Christian belief and religious practice.

Although I do not doubt the frequent influence of moral challenges and psychological factors in the so-called "loss of faith," my own feeling is that it is rash, if not outright insulting to many persons' integrity, to insist that all departures from the faith or from the church involve moral failure or perhaps even mental illness. The opposite may be true: a person's remaining in the church, even though that person's intellectual judgment—although we may consider it erroneous—dictates otherwise, can be a form of dishonesty, "bad faith," and hence hypocrisy. The regressions in faith that we spoke of in the preceding section could be a good example of the results of such compromise taking the place of honest doubt.

In this connection, the saying of Cardinal Newman is often cited, that "a thousand difficulties do not equal one doubt." True, if we mean by "doubt" a deliberate refusal to be open to faith, then we have to condemn such doubt. Nevertheless, the kind of persistent skepticism that many think of as "doubt" may paradoxically hide a deeper faith, in the existential sense of the word—a profound sense of commitment even in the face of intellectual uncertainty. Having faith does not mean avoiding tough questions, nor is holding to "the faith" identical with conforming to this or that school of theology.

If the Second Vatican Council admits that unbelievers, even atheists, are not excluded from God's saving grace, providing that they live according to their consciences (see *Lumen Gentium,* "The Constitution on the Church," Section 16), it seems logical that a former believer, particularly one whose faith had only reached the conventional stage, might reach the personal stage of self-commitment only in an apparently atheistic or humanistic form. This would most often occur in an environment where mature reflection on the faith was discouraged as being a dangerous questioning —a situation often found among communities that take refuge in a ghetto mentality. Or else it might happen where a supposedly progressive and scientific philosophy like Marxism seems the only alternative to what appears to be a corrupt and self-serving Christianity.

Part of this tendency, of course, is traceable to the old phenomenon of the grass appearing greener on the other side of the fence. Not only are the failures of organized religion down through the ages all too evident. It is always easier to appreciate the good points of another faith or system from afar and to compare them unfavorably with the defects of what one knows first-hand. We often see this in persons who idealize the eastern religions while rejecting their own western traditions.

In this regard it is also important to realize that the type of perfectionistic thinking that often inspires fanaticism as described in the previous section also has its role to play in the apparent loss or rejection of faith. Here the role of *conscience* remains critical.

In the wake of parental and ecclesiastical warnings, an over-developed and censorious conscience is apt to raise havoc, particularly when religious prohibitions against questioning belief and repeated admonitions to "take it on faith" have discouraged all serious reflective thought. Too often what is mistaken for conscience in the true sense of the word, an informed judgment leading to responsible action, is confused with the Freudian "super-ego," which is the internalized projection of the authoritarian parent. True conscience—understood in terms of its Latin roots meaning "with knowledge" or "awareness"—is something much more reasonable than these disturbing feelings that are often mistaken for the real thing.

Unfortunately, many people fail to make it through the transition to a truly personal faith because of this false or bad conscience which they suffer whenever they find themselves questioning some aspect of their old conventional faith. This leaves them caught between either irrationally holding on in what some ways amounts to bad faith or else giving up their faith altogether.

Those who would attempt to help people who are facing this critical stage must be ready to encourage and reassure them through this difficult process, as well as having achieved this level themselves. They must be ready, particularly if they in any way represent the authority associated with the previous stage, to be able to accept and absorb the ambivalence that the person is likely to display in the process. Such searchers after truth must not only be assured that questioning their previous faith is not sinful, but even more be encouraged to *continue* asking questions. The antagonism that so often characterizes those whose claim that they have "lost the faith" is most often traceable to their having only asked enough questions to justify, in *their* minds, their disbelief. What they have often failed to do is to follow through enough in their questioning to rebuild a faith of their own.

In some ways, terms such as "loss of faith" or "defection" from *the* faith are much too relative to be particularly helpful. What we should ask is whether such questioning or readiness to change beliefs represents a deepening of commitment. Here things are not always what they seem, and what sometimes appears to be an advance in faith may turn out to be, upon closer inspection, just the opposite.

Likewise we should be aware of the danger that "personal" or "individual" commitment might be confused with having a *private* religion. There is a distinct tendency, particularly because of modern individualism, to see one's faith commitment as a strictly private matter, between oneself and God alone. But this attitude, although readily understandable in the climate of American life (see particularly Robert Bellah, *Habits of the Heart: Individualism and Commitment in American Life*), and as a reaction to the "group" or social dimension of conventional faith, ignores some of the most obvious facts of basic psychology.

Personhood is largely a relational affair—one does not become a person apart from interaction with others. We may speak of different levels of the "self" and point out that "personhood" is largely a function of the "social self," but this does not mean that the so-called "ideal" or even the "real" or "higher" self can exist apart from our relation to others. But the illusion that one can have a strictly private faith or individual religion all one's own is a distinct danger, one that is similar to that facing persons who find themselves resisted in their attempts to grow—as families and societies often do resist change and those who attempt it. Often people will isolate themselves in an attempt to protect their own integrity. Again, this attitude is understandable in many young persons who feel the need to cut the apron strings that seem to bind them too closely to family and the society in which they were raised. Looked upon as part of the movement into personal faith, this rugged individualism in the growth of the life of faith is even excusable. But as a fixed or permanent state, it is unfortunate, and all too often represents the end of any further growth in faith.

When this happens it is a tremendous loss, not only for the society or community that needs to be prompted toward further growth precisely by individuals such as these, but also for the individuals themselves. The lack of personal commitment that so often arrests further spiritual growth frequently takes this form and in doing so violates the whole process of indirect fulfillment upon which growth depends. For if we are committed only to our *own* spiritual growth, how, in effect, are we to transcend ourselves? Frankl has warned us that the only *meaning* that can possibly ensure our happiness is bound up in a commitment to something or someone who is *greater* than ourselves, that goes *beyond* our selfish concern to have everything our own way.

As we shall see when it comes to our discussion of the higher levels of faith and spiritual growth, the greatest obstacle to progress is precisely bound up with the false idol of the perfect self. The image of the self-made saint, like that of the self-made millionaire, has a strong attraction for the person emerging from the cocoon of a conformist society and the womb of conventional faith. This temptation must be resisted. Not that we must not make our own choices, carry our own burdens, and trudge along our own path. No one else can do these things for us. But on the other hand, we must not shun our fellow pilgrims along the way, nor ignore the traditions and the wisdom of those who have gone before us. To do so would be to forget the most fundamental truth of all growth, that "unless the seed fall into the earth and die, it shall not bear fruit." Our isolated concern for self-perfection must first be dissolved in the earth of concern for others. Only then can it bear fruit "tenfold, sixtyfold, a hundredfold."

The Risk of Commitment

This dimension of involvement in the lives of others brings us back to the question of "implicit conversion" raised by Babin in his book (pp. 65–70). Not all conversions are as explicit as the formal, conscious decision made either for or against God. Instead many people do not live under circumstances in which they are forced to deliberately make such a choice. Yet sooner or later, most people are confronted with some other choice in life that demands personal commitment; this choice usually revolves around some issue of social or interpersonal involvement, marriage, a particular vocation, or the like. And implicit in this involvement are (according to Babin) four elements:

(1) Allegiance to a creed and morality;
(2) Adherence to certain practices;
(3) Loyalty to certain structures, institutions, people;
(4) Adherence to certain deep-seated principles. (Babin, p. 67)

On the surface, such a cluster of loyalties could represent no more than simply the practice of a merely conventional faith. But appearances may be deceiving. What may appear to be simply a "conventional faith" in the sense of mere conformity to the socio-cultural patterns of society may still involve a real element of personal commitment that raises it above mere conformism. We must not be too quick to judge. "Good faith" in the sense of personal integrity may often co-exist with certain elements of "bad faith" as understood in the existentialist sense or with a faith structure which alienates the believer from authentic involvement in life.

The weaknesses of faith that are bound up with such implicit conversions are of two kinds, according to Babin (p. 69). One is the result of implicit conversion "*without adequate reflection,*" which may lead to a strong commitment but defective understanding of that to which they are committed. In such a case there is a strong element of moral determination but an intellectual shakiness—probably a major factor in the kinds of regressions described earlier in this chapter.

On the other hand, Babin also describes implicit conversions that lack "*a vital and deliberate decision.*" All the knowledge and understanding are there, and they *do* seem to have some effect on the believer's orientation to life, but they never seem to make a really decisive difference. The commitment itself seems less than total, and, as Babin adds, such implicit decisions, with the same flaws, are often seen in the case of a lapse from faith. (Here one is reminded of the warning in the New Testament book of Revelation 3:15–16 against being "neither hot or cold" and its consequences.)

Similar to these forms of implicit conversion—or is it perhaps just another way of looking at the same thing?— Babin describes "conversion (or lapse) through the ratification of a given situation" (pp. 70–72). People often make choices in life without the full awareness of the consequences. Babin uses marriage and its effect on religious practice as the most obvious example. Immaturity, naiveté, or the lack of preparedness for the demands of marriage or of one's chosen profession or vocation will occasion a crisis. And out of the confrontation there are (again) three possible resolutions: outright rejection of the situation (divorce in the one case or apostasy in the other), running away or withdrawal from the conflict (putting off the decision, distraction, denial), or, finally, ratification or recommitment.

All this brings to mind Gabriel Marcel's existential distinction between "choosing" and "willing," again with marriage as an obvious example. A couple falls in love, and they *choose* each other as an intended life partner, but it is only in the course of time, after they truly know each other, as well as become more fully aware of the other options they might have had, that they can be said to truly *will* their fidelity to each other. Is not the same true of our faith commitment? Anyone can choose a "faith" in the sense of a series of beliefs, but it is only in the face of a test of willed commitment that a person is forced to finally confront the ultimate meaning of one's life and to act upon it.

This is not to disparage so-called "implicit conversions" or those that have come about mostly through force of circumstances. Indeed, most choices in life are probably made this way—including those involved in an "explicit conversion." In some way, because of the immediacy of their practical consequences, such implicit conversions underline the necessity for the existential *commitment* that characterizes a truly personal faith. The levels of intellectual understanding, moral reasoning, and the other criteria that are built into Fowler's depiction of the faith stages are all important, often vitally so for consistency in each stage, but above all it is the component of decisive commitment on which the claim to have a truly personal faith stands or falls. Without it, we may have a sophisticated religious worldview, but we really don't have "faith" in the full sense of the word. And where there is this commitment, we have the real nucleus of faith, no matter how theologically naive or otherwise misshapen this commitment might be.

This of course brings with it tremendous risk. And with the growing awareness of the risk comes a growing sense of *insecurity*. What appears to be "a bridge over troubled waters" turns out to lack handrails, and what seemed easy at first—as long as one kept one's attention on the opposite shore—becomes unnerving as soon as one is forced to turn one's attention to what lies beneath. No wonder that many retreat in panic or else cling as one paralyzed to whatever consoling plank or other handhold that is available, even if it points back in the wrong direction. Babin (p. 133) cites psychiatrist Karen Horney's diagnosis of "anxiety [being] the disease of our time." This observation, along with Frankl's opinion that over fifty percent of all mental illness could be termed "existential neurosis"—traceable directly to a lack of "meaning" in a person's life—should make us doubly aware of the crucial necessity of faith as an essential foundation for human life. It should also make us aware in our times of the particular susceptibility of religious faith to various forms of distortion, particularly by those who use it to exploit people's sense of insecurity.

Conclusion

After looking at these problems connected with the emergence of personal faith, we may well wonder if it is worth the struggle and the dangers involved. If the dangers, particularly of the excesses of fanaticism on the one hand, or of apparent loss of faith on the other, are so great, one may well dread the possible outcome. We are reminded of the gospel warning that "having swept out seven devils . . . the last state may become worse than the first" (Mt 12:49; Lk 11:26). Religious leaders down through the centuries have been only too well aware of these dangers, and more often than not have been tempted to restrict growth in this direction lest, as they say, "the faithful be scandalized."

So let there be no doubt about it, there are genuine risks connected with the emergence of truly committed, personal faith. But the greatest risk, by far, is not that the process of achieving a personal faith will go astray in some such manner, but that it will never begin at all.

Questions for Reflection and Discussion

1. Your college sophomore returns home on vacation. He or she announces to your shocked family that he or she is convinced that religion is a lot of superstition and that the only honest position is to be an atheist. How do you handle this one?

2. At what age did you first experience difficulties or doubt about "the faith"? What doctrine(s) were they about? How did you resolve them?

3. Knowing what you do now, at what age do you think the sacrament of confirmation should be received? Give your reasoning for your position.

4. Have you had anything like a "conversion" experience in your life? In what sense of the word (conversion)? When or how did it occur?

5. In what way do you see faith as a risk?

7. Conjunctive Faith

There is no light without shadow and no psychic wholeness without imperfection. To round itself out, life calls not for perfection but for completeness; and for this the "thorn in the flesh" is needed, the suffering of defects without which there is no progress and no ascent.

> C.G. Jung, *Psychology and Alchemy*

More than from any other author, this quotation from the great modern psychiatrist Carl Gustave Jung seems in order here. One reason that I shied away from Fowler's terminology for the previous stage is that *"individuation,"* as this movement toward completeness was termed by Jung, better describes the process that distinctively characterizes this more advanced "conjunctive faith."

After first calling it "paradoxical-consolidative faith," Fowler decided to use this single word, *conjunctive*, which of course implies a "joining together"—in this case a conjoining of all those elements into that unique combination that constitutes this or that individual person. Accordingly, in his later book, Fowler describes this conjunctive faith:

> ... the stage of faith that emerges with mid-life or beyond involves the integration of elements in ourselves, in society, and in our experience of ultimate reality that have the character of apparent contradictions, polarities, or at least paradoxical elements. (Fowler, 1984 p. 64)

As such this movement is, in effect, what Jung understood as "individuation" and which must not be confused, as we have seen, with "individualism" understood as a strictly personal affair, self-centered and without reference to others except to mark differences between us. Mere individualism, if it retains any spiritual aspects at all, too often becomes a kind of private religion marked by negativity—a rejection of one's cultural, familiar, and often even personal past.

Such a negative or critical attitude, as we have seen, is often a preliminary step, just as the more positive second phase, the so-called "conversion," or arrival at a personal faith, also marks the *beginning* of the maturing process. Still, to become a truly *mature* believer the individual person has a long way to go.

Personal Integration and Conjunctive Faith

In many ways, the process of maturation must move in the opposite direction from that taken by the young person seeking his or her own identity. Where, before, the movement was often away from what one had been in the effort to seek new ideals and goals, now the movement is marked most of all by an attempt to reintegrate, to reappropriate, and to come to terms with the past in a way that extracts the good from all that went before.

Instead of the tendency toward one-sided fanaticism often present in a newly discovered personal faith, or the defensiveness that marks too long or too rigid an adherence to one's own personal or even private faith, conjunctive faith will show a new appreciation of others and a new-found respect for their beliefs and views. Tolerance for diversity is one mark of a maturing faith.

Another hallmark is patience with oneself. The longer one lives the more one understands why "Rome was not built in a day." We discover, often to our dismay, that certain elements in our personality (St. Paul's "thorn in the flesh") just don't disappear by our simply willing it, and that we can't build a whole new self by wishful thinking. Indeed, the "new you" will always turn out to be the recycled you, preferably in a new improved version. Like the "before and after" snapshots touting muscle-building machines or weight-loss salons, we might approach the project with high hopes, but however hard we work at it, the results, at best, are apt to be disappointingly limited.

Another way of putting this is to recall the old theological adage that "grace builds upon nature." Divine help improves on what is already there. It rarely destroys anything, seldom touching the roots of the passions and drives that we have allowed to lead us astray. Instead, grace heals, redirects energies, purifies motives.

In addition, our thought processes must become more integrated. Earlier black and white, either/or style of thinking slowly gives way to *both* (on the one hand) *and* (on the other), or a "not only but also" type of approach to problem solving and thinking. We learn to avoid supposedly simple solutions for everything in the face of the complexity of reality in all its fullness—and this includes the complexity of our own nature as well.

Another way of looking at this stage is proposed by Richard Sweeney when he calls this faith "mystical." I do not feel that this is a good title because it might imply that the person reaching this stage is a mystic—and there are just too many arguments about and too many attempts to define what exactly "mysticism" is for it to be very helpful. Still, this stage of faith draws from the common fund of mystical insight, which is to say that faith at this stage has reached a new appreciation of the core values and insights that exist within all religions, despite the apparent diversity and disagreements. It is also "mystical" in the sense that it is reached when people begin to get in touch with the deeper aspects of their personality and the elements of divine grace working within them.

If I were to add one other adjective to the description of this stage of faith, I would call it "holistic faith," for much the same reasons. One need not be an accomplished mystic, or even a born one, to have a basic sense of the *whole*. But at the same time, one is not apt to have much of this sensitivity unless one is respectful of the whole of one's own past life and upbringing, as well as the whole of one's own personality, the unconscious as well as the conscious, body as well as soul, emotions as well as intellect. The dualistic thinking found in much of religious thought in various ways (good vs. evil, light vs. darkness, spirit vs. matter, etc.) has its proper function, no doubt, but it is not characteristic of maturing, holistic, conjunctive faith, nor, one might add, "monotheistic" faith—since, ultimately, *everything* must be traced to one God. As faith matures, a new emphasis on the whole, the global, the universal, surfaces. In some ways, it might be described as movement toward "catholic" thinking in the original sense of the word or phrase—*kath/kata* as "toward" or "into" or "serving" the *holos* or whole. Without this sense of, and some achievement of, this wholeness, it is difficult to see where genuine holiness can exist, at least in the form that God fully intended it to be.

When Fowler first termed this faith stage as "paradoxical-consolidative," it was because he wished to stress the task of learning how to make sense of all the paradoxes or contradictions within ourselves and to come to terms with them, and to combine their strengths or to consolidate the pluses while trying to minimize the effects of the minuses. But this is not a process that can be carried on merely *within* our isolated selves. As we shall soon see, a conjunctive faith is also a faith that is in dialogue with others.

But first we must ask how this stage is usually reached. Psychologically speaking, a major ingredient is simply the process of maturation in itself. To truly mature, persons must generally incorporate *all*, or most, of the elements, experiences, trials or whatever else that has contributed to their personhood or being. This means that no significant part of oneself or one's personal history can be repressed— even one's mistakes and failures. To do so would mean to cut off not only the vital sources of energy but also the wisdom that was, or should have been, gained even when these forces may have been misused. The price of repression is distortion, and any significant denial of this kind will result in the atrophy of one or another facet of the personality.

Much the same is true regarding our environmental history or background. One's socio-cultural roots cannot ever be abandoned entirely, or not without an obvious deformation occurring as a result. Although one may arrive at the point of appearing fully adapted to a new environment—not just speaking a new language, for example, but even thinking in it—still, the denial of the subtle and residual influences of the past, even if only for the purposes of resisting them, will most likely result in a lopsidedness that is apparent to all except to the person engaged in this denial. What happens so often in such cases is that the person's new identity is bound to exhibit the more obvious faults associated with the purely individualized "personal faith" stage, such as exaggerated dichotomies in reasoning and the lack of tolerance and sensitivity that such thinking often exhibits.

Conjunctive faith, on the other hand, exhibits a reasoning process that is more fully dialectical. Although dialectic, of course, begins in the contrasting of apparent opposites and often seems *paradoxical* or outright contradictory, it is able to rise above them in the classic pattern of *thesis* vs. *antithesis* resolved in *synthesis*. For example, take the long-standing contrast between God viewed as transcendent (or, popularly speaking, "outside of" creation) and divinity as immanent (or contained "within" creation). The synthesis, of course, is not a compromise that says God is "partly inside" of and partly "outside of" the universe, but in a realization that we are talking about a subject that itself transcends or goes beyond such physical categories. Hence, *meta*physically speaking, God is *both* or, as St. Thomas Aquinas put it, God can be fully immanent within creation only because God is completely transcendent.

I have used this example because "transcendence" is, in more than one sense, a key word here. In terms of a person's moral or ethical reasoning, the conjunctive stage involves an ability to see issues from a variety of perspectives and not just from that which is determined by one's own socio-cultural or religious tradition. This means that one must have extended the horizon of one's own awareness far beyond local and invariably limited and often selfish concerns. This also means that one has gained an education of some sort, if not formally, maybe through travel or simply by living long enough. Exposure to reality as perceived and experienced by others almost invariably brings about a change of perspective.

Such a broadening of horizons should result in a corresponding deepening of one's own moral views. Typically, it leads to a quest for ethical wisdom in a form that we already (Chapter 4) have spoken of as "natural law." While the prophets spoke of this as a law "written in the heart," St. Paul argues that it should have been so obvious that even the pagan world had no excuse for ignoring it (compare with the book of Wisdom 13:1–9 and Romans 1:18ff). Accordingly, the same concept was present in the Greek world in the form of such ideas as that of an eternal *Logos* or "mind" or "reason" (or in Oriental thought, the *Tao* or "Way") that is identified with the first cause of all things. This "mind" or "way" is the origin of and the pattern for an inherent order in nature. Hence, a conjunctive faith usually includes a rational ethical perspective that reflects a deep knowledge of human nature and nature at large, of history, and a sympathetic understanding of many religious and ethical systems as well.

In such a perspective, of course, the "locus of authority" becomes largely impersonal. Even though in Christian theology the *Logos* takes personal form—following the personification of wisdom in the Hebrew scriptures—still this divine "reason" tends to become more abstract, not to be remote, but to become more universally embodied in human institutions that must transcend socio-cultural and, particularly, religious differences. Things are seen as right or wrong not because God or some other authority has said so, but because of a basic wisdom and rationality that is inherent in divinity itself.

Another very important and significant shift in thinking patterns characterizes this stage—one that at first glance may seem a regression to an earlier stage. *Symbol* is rediscovered and reintegrated as the language *par excellence* of faith. Having been "broken" from a naive literalism of the earliest stages of belief and divested of its multi-layered socio-cultural trappings that characterize conventional faith, "myth" now reemerges as a privileged means of not only expressing *existential truth*—truths that never "happened" as historical events but that simply "are"—but also as a means of interreligious and intercultural understanding. The reason that myth is able to do this in a way that even scientific theology is unable to is because it remains *multidimensional*—which means that the story can be understood on several levels at the same time. In other words, it is precisely because of its ability to handle paradoxes and to conjoin them that myth and the language of symbol are now revitalized with new and much deeper meaning.

In sum, conjunctive faith represents both an advance beyond and yet, paradoxically, a renewed appreciation for and a reappropriation of much that was cast aside when a person moved from the phases of faith that tend to characterize childhood to forge an individualized personal faith of one's own. Just as the idealism of adolescence, which can be generally very hard and demanding, even rejecting, of one's former ways, needs to be corrected by the mellowing influence of a mature adult life, so too the enthusiasms and often rigid convictions of a personal but still-maturing faith need to be tempered by a reclaiming of what was valid in the past into a new synthesis for the present. In this way, conjunctive faith becomes a more truly mature faith, even though it is

still not the ultimate, and still must struggle with the ambi-
guities and conflicting polarities that afflict the human condition.

Some of these polarities are experienced most deeply
within ourselves, seemingly in isolation from the rest of the
world. For some, the risk of faith is primarily an existential,
deeply personal thing. Undoubtedly, there can be no final
evasion of the challenge of making a here and now and
ultimately personal, individual choice. That being said—and
we will soon return to that topic—something else also must
be said as well. Choices, no matter how personal, are never
made in a vacuum, completely isolated from the world
around us. This is even more true on the level of conjunctive
faith. The struggle to achieve a personal faith amidst all the
pushes and tugs exerted by childhood loyalties and the conventions of society was difficult enough. Now we have to
face all this again, but in a new, integrating rather than rejecting way.

Ecumenical Faith

From looking at the difficulties involved in arriving at a
conjunctive faith in terms of the individual's life, we now
turn toward the ecclesial or communal dimensions of conjunctive faith. Simply put, a conjunctive faith is necessarily
an *ecumenical* faith. But just as the meaning of the Greek
word *oikumene,* originally referring to a family or house-
hold, eventually was extended to include the clan or tribe,
and later the whole human race, so our modern theological
notion of ecumenism has likewise grown. In its most restricted sense, the word usually refers to the efforts toward
cooperation and union between the various Christian
churches or denominations. But more broadly taken, it must
ultimately refer to finding a path to harmony between the
world's major faiths.

Understood in either sense, ecumenical thinking, far

from being a peripheral concern, must be seen not only as an essential, but also as *the* single most important element in the maturing process. Conversely, it might be added, the success of the efforts of ecumenism as a movement depends largely on those concerned with arriving at a conjunctive level of faith. So both the achievement of a personally conjunctive level of faith and the success of ecumenical thinking are mutually dependent. One will not occur without the other, or if by chance the semblance of one does occur in the absence of the other, it will soon prove to be extremely limited and without any deep effect on life as really lived, whether it be in the life of the individual believer or the collective life of a church.

For example, while merely "conventional faith" presents a distinct opportunity, it also presents a distinct problem for ecumenical efforts. Unlike the mentality often found in those of "literal faith," conventional faith, despite its tendency toward narrow parochialism and preserving the *status quo,* retains a certain openness to community and social cooperation—at least in our pluralistic society—that, if approached carefully, may allow for corporate movements toward reunion. But still, if the socio-cultural dynamics of this stage are not understood thoroughly, great miscalculations can occur. A careful understanding of this stage must always keep us aware that faith, no matter how much it may become "individuated," still normally has its psycho-social roots and, to some degree, even its theological underpinnings (in terms of divine providence) in a community of believers. To expect people to readily let go of their own confessional differences or traditional ways of expressing their faith would be to make the fatal mistake of asking them to disown their identity. The current argument over the extent of permitted religious "inculturalization" in the former mission churches of the third world is, in this respect, an ecumenical issue which can be solved only in terms of a conjunctive faith that is able to leave room for local versions of what amounts to conventional faith.

When we come to the level of a more personal faith, the situation becomes somewhat reversed. Aside from those who fall prey to the born-again enthusiasms which are often opposed to ecumenism, people in this stage of faith are quite capable of exhibiting an ecumenical enthusiasm that can take the movement a long way, particularly by way of active commitment. But they can only do so effectively if they begin to understand some of the limitations and pitfalls of their own inner dynamic. Mere enthusiasm can do more damage than good.

So we must conclude that ecumenical leaders must themselves be, by and large, people of a conjunctive faith. We cannot expect ecumenical initiative to come from the ranks of the merely conventional. While stronger initiatives may be taken by persons whose personal faith has made them real instruments of grace for others, the very strength of their own convictions can often polarize others whose own journey of reflection and commitment may have taken a quite different path. Somehow the truly effective ecumenical leader has to combine the enthusiasm of the true believer with the social awareness of conventional religiosity, not to strike a compromise between them, but to transcend both.

The necessity of a conjunctive faith approach can also be seen in the debate over what form a unified Christianity would take. Too often union is thought of in terms of uniformity, especially in doctrinal matters, while others see it primarily as a matter of "confessional" style—even while there is basic doctrinal agreement. History shows that Christianity has always contained a certain amount of diversity and theological pluralism, even in the New Testament scriptures themselves. This is something that those who have not reached a conjunctive level of faith find difficult to deal with. Instead they typically lay down conditions first before they will engage in dialogue, rather than trust the Spirit enough to let the desire for union lead the way. No doubt there are painful issues to be faced. No one has ever promised that marriages do not sometimes involve pain. So it is with the efforts toward Christian unity—real sacrifice is often called for from everyone involved.

For leader or follower alike, ecumenism brings with it the challenge to grow in our faith. The prayer of Jesus that all his disciples "be one, Father . . . as you are in me and I am in you" (Jn 17:12) can only come about if we are willing to follow his great command to "love one another as I have loved you" and to prove to the world that there is "no greater love than to lay down one's life for one's friend" (see Jn 15:12–13). The sin and scandal of Christian disunity, while it often poses as "fidelity" to the word of God, is more often just the opposite.

Nevertheless, most Christians seem to accept these divisions as being realistic or inevitable, even while remaining an unfortunate barrier to the conversion of those "sheep" who "are not of this fold" and thus preventing Jesus' stated wish that there may be "one flock and one shepherd" (as given in Jn 10:16) and that ". . . they all be one, Father; may they be one in us, as you are in me and I am in you, so that the world may believe that it was you who sent me" (see Jn 17:21).

But I wonder if these passages are read too often exclusively with an eye to "conversion" as the spreading of the Christian religion throughout the world. No doubt, Christian disunity is a barrier to the spread of the faith. But if we stop here we miss the point. Ecumenism is not merely a tool for conversion. Instead, unity is a major goal not for Christianity's sake. Instead the goal of *all* religion is unity—unity of the human with the divine and the unity of all humanity. So ecumenism is not simply one movement among others, to be accomplished through a series of tactics, dialogues, etc.

Unity itself is *the* goal which at the same time is the principal way as well. The whole purpose of Christianity, according to the Johannine theology, is to replicate among Christians, and thus invite *all* humanity to share in that same unity that exists between the Father and the Son. So too, in the Pauline understanding of Christianity, the ultimate goal is that redeemed humanity, one with Christ, is made one with the Father. Thus "we are Christ's and Christ is God's" (1 Cor 3:23) so that, in the end, "God may become all in all" (1 Cor 15:28) *NAB*.

But if it is granted that Christian unity is more than just a means to an end, what stands in its way? Underneath all the doctrinal divisions and other excuses, it is ultimately our unwillingness to let go of ourselves and "let God be God" in our lives. The divine grace or initiative is not lacking, but rather our own resolve is deficient. The only real question is, then: Do we really want this unity to come about?

When we really come down to it, at the heart of the ecumenical problem it is ultimately a question of letting go of an imagined *security* to take the *risk* of pure faith and trust in God, stripped of the illusory support of dogmatic principles and institutional props. Not that Christian faith will not express itself in certain convictions or "beliefs"— the revelation of God through and in Jesus being central. But this faith must concretely embody itself in church or community, for how else can we even begin to express the unity Jesus enjoined upon us? Yet our adherence to the teaching or our loyalty to the community cannot be allowed to stand in opposition to our basic commitment to God.

We sometimes forget that Jesus did not come to found another "religion." Instead, he came rather to call *all* people —even though first of all his own Jewish people—to a closer union with God and to be instruments of God's will on earth. It is only to the extent that his followers have failed to accomplish this that we can speak of "Christianity" as a "religion" opposed to other religions, or, even worse, separate Christian "churches" as institutional entities that somehow are rivals to each other.

Thus Christian ecumenism, as a communal expression of conjunctive faith, can only come about in an atmosphere of *risk,* a risking of self-identity, a risking of institutional pride, and a genuine sacrifice of self in love. This implies that the various Christian churches or communities as we know them are in some way called to *self-transcendence,* to be prepared to apparently lose themselves and their own self-identity in the interest of that greater "communion" willed by God in Christ. There is no other way. But if this is the case within Christianity and the conjunctive faith which is demanded of it, what is to be said about its total relationship to the world and especially to the other religions in the world?

Raising this whole question of ecumenism on a global scale in the broader sense of the relationship of Christianity to the rest of the world's religions is a good way to bring on a panic attack. Many otherwise ecumenically-minded Christians stop short at this point. Ecumenism, they feel, has its limits. Unity between Christians—yes! But unity or some kind of convergence between all the world's believers?

While our consideration of conjunctive faith seems to demand that this wider view of ecumenism be confronted at this point, I have decided to postpone our consideration of it until after the next chapter on "universalizing" or, as I prefer to call it, "unitive" faith. One of my reasons for doing so will not become apparent until we take the time necessary to consider at much more length the kind of interior transformation that has to take place before one can begin to fully appreciate the deeper unity that lies behind the wide divergences within the world's major religions.

But there is another, more immediate reason for stopping short on this topic at this point. It has to do with the dangers of openness and the nature of risk itself.

Openness or Indifference?

To many people who may have arrived at a strongly committed and truly personal faith, the person who claims to have arrived at a "conjunctive" faith may appear to be somewhat vague, relativistic, or altogether uncommitted. What may seem like a healthy dose of reverent agnosticism to some may seem like outright "wishy-washiness" to others. If so, the judgment, however rash, may be not far off the mark, in view of what is the most common temptation at this stage—a situation which, at least in the beginning, may sometimes take on the appearance of a mid-life crisis of faith.

The perspective-taking that involves the ability to see other persons' point of view, or to take into account cultural and historical factors different from our own, or even to accept one's own failures with some equanimity—all these may produce an impression that is frustrating and puzzling for the person who thinks of faith in terms of unshakable absolutes, unassailable dogmas, and ready answers for every possible moral dilemma. To the contrary, for the person possessing a more conjunctive faith, such sureness may appear to be a suspicious over-simplification.

Of course, the impression that the more self-assured, personally-committed believer may have might just be correct; the person aspiring to have this conjunctive faith may actually have very little faith of any sort. Although they may claim to be able to see the value of all faiths or beliefs, their broad-minded tolerance may serve to mask their lack of commitment to any serious practice of faith in the concrete challenges of life. They may even go so far as to brand any commitment, other than to their own carefully cultivated broad-mindedness, as fanaticism or narrow-thinking. They want to be above all that. So sometimes what might appear to be a conjunctive faith may turn out to be a disguise for no faith at all.

It is not too difficult to understand the cause of such an attitude, particularly when it can pose as academic objectivity. The serious comparative study of religions, or even of the "phenomenology of religion"—to take such study to another level—does require, to some extent, that a person lay aside his or her own personal commitments, at least in a theoretical sense, in order to "bracket" or stand aside from one's own belief system (or to put it into parentheses, so to speak) to try to enter the mental world of someone else whose belief system may differ radically from one's own. Thus you cannot possibly expect to even begin to understand Vedic (Hindu) religion if you remain tied to western categories of thought. You have to try to enter, as fully as possible, into the world-view of a completely alien culture —something that may be, in the long run, quite impossible. Jung, for one, especially in his *Psychology and Religion: West and East* (Collected Works, II) repeatedly warned about the dangers of such well-intentioned but often superficial attempts. Nevertheless, we must try to bridge the gap.

Openness to the views and beliefs of others does not necessarily mean that we accept them uncritically. Instead it simply means that we develop the ability to place ourselves in another person's shoes or situation and to be able to sympathetically attempt to understand where they are coming from and appreciate the values which their approach affords. Through this process we can hope to gain some new insights for ourselves, some of them resulting in a deepened appreciation for and understanding of forgotten elements of our own religious tradition. To accomplish this, however, means that we have to be able, at least to some degree, to step out of our own mental habits, and in the process setting aside, as it were, our own beliefs temporarily so as to try to enter another person's world. This is, of course, almost completely impossible for persons of conventional faith, since their whole mentality is dominated by their conformity to their own culture and its thinking. But it is almost as difficult for people of intensely personal faith as well. They are apt to be so strongly committed to their own set of beliefs that even the idea of another person being satisfied by another set of beliefs is incomprehensible—yet underneath they are not sure of themselves enough to be able to try to understand another point of view without feeling threatened by it.

Of course, the question of whether this "bracketing" can ever be completely accomplished, even by one who aspires to a conjunctive faith, is something else. Most likely the best that can be accomplished is to try to keep this openness in mind as a prerequisite for a serious and sympathetic study of another's religion. But at the same time we must remember that the loss of commitment to one's own beliefs—which amounts to the refusal to commit oneself to the ultimate as one discovers it—removes any possibility of entering into religious experience at its deepest level. In other words, bracketing one's own belief is not the same as suspending one's own commitment. Furthermore, the attempt to abstract oneself from one's own bias will fail, paradoxically, to the extent that one imagines that one has completely succeeded. One can learn all about religions or even a particular set of beliefs without ever having faith. At the best, that person's appreciation and knowledge remain second-hand; at the worst an uncommitted aloofness can lose the meaning of the whole thing.

All this is not to say that an academic or studious approach does not play a necessary and crucial role. But the open-mindedness and sympathy that characterize conjunctive faith should not be too easily identified with the supposedly neutral objectivity that is the ideal of much of the academic world. To the contrary, these two attitudes are quite the opposite despite some surface similarities. Because conjunctive faith is the result of the integration of different levels of or aspects of our being, it is able not only to assimilate paradoxical truths—such as God understood as transcendent as well as immanent—but also to incorporate seemingly conflicting commitments.

Thus conjunctive faith sees no real contradiction between a sympathetic understanding of all religions, coupled with a deep commitment to one's own faith. It realizes that human reason and logic have their limitations, and is able to live with the greater mystery that transcends all human knowledge. At the same time, such a faith seeks to integrate all knowledge, for example, convinced that there can be no real conflict between science and religion, between reason and faith, since it believes that the same God is the origin of both. But it is respectful of the rules that govern each. It sees them as complementary, but not identical ways of approaching reality.

In sum, conjunctive faith recognizes that even if we must first "believe in order to understand," still faith that fails to go on to greater understanding is a very dangerous thing. Again Jung warns us:

> Understanding is never the handmaiden of faith—on the contrary, faith completes understanding. To educate men to a faith they do not understand is certainly a well meant undertaking, but one that runs the risk of creating an attitude that believes everything it does not understand. (C.G. Jung, *Marginalia on Contemporary Events* ["On the Reeducation of the Germans," 1946], Collected Works 18)

A truly conjunctive faith must fully integrate commitment with an expanded knowledge. That in itself is not an easy task, and for those with a weak understanding of their own beliefs or a shaky commitment, the task may be quite beyond their capabilities. But as great as these risks may be in coming to a conjunctive level of faith, there is, at least for some, an even greater risk.

The Risk of Risking

If we were to ask what is the single *greatest,* if not the most common, danger in this conjunctive faith stage, our answer itself would also have to take something of the form of a seeming contradiction. The paradoxical nature of conjunctive faith contains a temptation that is more subtle than simply the lure of uncommitted openness. If the risk of unreasoned literal or conventional faith is credulousness, and the risk in the effort to come to a personal faith is either to become a fanatic or else end up with no faith at all, the greatest risk in achieving conjunctive faith is the peculiar one of succumbing to the attraction of *risk for its own sake* —a problem not unlike that of the compulsive gambler, someone who has, for whatever reason, a pathological addiction to risk.

Back in Chapter 2, I spoke particularly about "existential" faith. This modern emphasis on commitment in the face of uncertainty highlights the risk of faith, particularly when faith no longer seems to be bolstered by the traditions and convictions that both undergirded and expressed the faith of past ages. What seemed like clear evidence proving the existence of God, of divine providence, of creative wisdom—much of this has been called into question in modern times. It seems like modern persons are forced to have a lot more faith commitment than "medieval man" had when the convictions appeared to be so self-evident—or so we imagine. To a large extent the modern hero of faith is the person who commits himself or herself without knowing, who hopes against hope despite the lack of evidence that would make belief a sure thing.

Perhaps this is why, among other things, we can trace an evolution of the meaning of the word "believe" from primarily an affective emphasis (close to its root in the Germanic word for "love") to the present intellectual and volitional stress on our holding something to be true despite a lack of much evidence. Even Jung implied this, when he pointed out:

> No one can know what the ultimate things are. We must therefore take them as we experience them. And if such an experience helps to make life healthier, more beautiful, more complete, and more satisfactory to yourself and those you love, you may safely say: "This was the grace of God." No transcendental truth is thereby demonstrated, and we must confess in all humility that religious experience is *extra ecclesiam* [outside the church], subjective, and liable to boundless error! (C.G. Jung, *Psychology and Religion*, Collected Works 74, 1938).

Is this existential faith or is it simply naive willfulness or wishful thinking? For most, it would constitute a certain stubborn refusal to take "no" for an answer to the riddle of life's meaning, despite the lack of hard evidence. To some, such an attitude is nothing less than heroic, for despite the demands of such a faith, the rewards seem slim. How much more accommodating seems the conclusion of Dostoyevsky who observed that "without God, everything is possible."

To others, such existential faith seems childish. How much more straightforward and honest is Nietzsche's anti-hero, Zarathustra, who boldly proclaimed that "God is dead —we have killed him!" Truly, now all is permitted, provided we have the courage to take responsibility into our own hands. Yet rightly understood, and not perversely as Hitler twisted it, Nietzsche's proclamation was not meant to be an invitation to immorality but instead a summons for pure humanitarian goodness with no hope or desire for reward in this world or the next.

But for some others, even this skeptical attitude would not be without hope, for *if* there is a God, and he "rewards and punishes," then can't we reasonably expect that this God will reward a life lived unselfishly *despite* (or even more unselfishly *because of*) the lack of certainty about what's in it for us? So argued the seventeenth century Jansenist philosopher Blaise Pascal. Why not believe in God in the face of uncertainty and act accordingly? If there is no God, what *really* would you have lost? But if there is a God, and you have not acted rightly, you *could* end by losing everything.

Some may see in Pascal's famous "wager" not just a shrewd but even a cynical calculation and not worth serious consideration, particularly if we believe God rewards only those who are sincere. But actually it makes a lot of sense to someone of conventional faith—which can be quite sincere in its own way. People will respect you, and even if there is no life after death, you'll miss nothing of really great importance—including hell, for there wouldn't be that possibility either. But if there turns out to be such life, God will accept you, maybe even specially reward you, for being such an upright character in the face of all this uncertainty. And there are added perks as well. You can always tell yourself that God can hardly blame you for not doing more in the face of so much insecurity, so your commitment needn't really be outstanding. So there is even a certain amount of *security* to be had in assuming this modern sort of risk— whatever you do (short of being an absolute cad) will assure, or at least not interfere with, any future possibilities that God may hold in store. It is the best of all possible worlds—yes, you can have your cake and eat it too.

Of course, such calculating risk, not for risk's but really for one's own sake, is really the inverse of a personally committed faith. If there is any self-forgetfulness involved, it is not unlike the pseudo-transcendence of any of the false goals that we humans often use to while away our time.

On the contrary, a truly *conjunctive* faith will see

through Pascal's cool analysis of the odds which deceptively mask the utter riskiness of faith. Against the bourgeoise calculation to enjoy the best of both worlds the truly existential choice that a *committed* faith involves, as against a merely self-pleasing "aesthetic choice"—to borrow Søren Kierkegaard's terminology—is a choice that demands that we put our lives where our good intentions claim to be. In a world filled with suffering and injustice, there can be no excuse. Do we really think God will be taken for such a fool?

Here we are brought back to Frankl's criticism, not of the pleasure-principle of Freudian psychology, but of the power-principle of the Adlerian school. The modern pop-psychologies talk bravely of "risking" and "venturing," of "affirmation" and "self-actualization"—all fine and brave words, taken as *means* but not ends in themselves. When joined to worthy goals, they serve a worthwhile function. But joined to self-centered aims or as a posturing of ourselves in the role of "modern existential man," they are but slogans for an ego-trip.

Conclusion

Our consideration of "conjunctive faith" has led us to what appears to be the very limits of faith in any usual sense of the term. We are brought to full confrontation with the paradox that lies at the heart of all genuine faith. For if one would consistently apply the challenge of the gospels that "to save one's life in this world" is to lose it, while "to lose one's life . . . is to save it" (see Mk 8:35–37 and parallels, Mt 16:25–26; Lk 9:24; 17:33), then it would follow that to live the life of faith one must be ready to sacrifice all the sureness and the security it promises. It almost seems that without the commitment to living insecurely, any claim to be living by or in faith disappears. Of itself this situation points toward a state beyond.

Questions for Reflection and Discussion

1. Why, in your opinion (or in your experience), is it unlikely that a "conjunctive" faith will occur before the onset of midlife? If it did occur earlier, would this be a good thing? Why or why not?
2. Discuss, from as many angles you can think of, the possible meanings or variations of a saying like "the various churches or religions are just different roads to the same goal." In what ways would you agree or disagree with this statement or its variations?
3. To what extent do you think education is a threat to religion? Or to what extent do you think lack of education is a threat to personal belief?
4. How would you describe the "existential risk" element of faith in your own life? Where exactly are the risks? What concrete shape does the commitment take?

8. Unitive Faith

The temptation of Conjunctive faith ... is to become immobilized in its compassion. The polarities of its loves and loyalties can seem to cancel each other. Persons of Conjunctive faith long for transforming newness; yet their integrity involves keeping steadfast commitments to institutions and persons in the present. They see the possibility, even the imperative, of lives lived in solidarity with *all* being. Yet their wills, affections, and actions manifest tension, division, and disunity. Being in, but not of the world, they feel a cosmic homelessness and loneliness. For some, this longing and discomfort become the means by which they are called and lured into a transformed and transforming relationship to the ultimate conditions of life—and to themselves and everyday existence with the neighbor. This transforming and transformed relation we call Universalizing faith.

James W. Fowler, *Becoming Adult,*
Becoming Christian

This final "universalizing" stage of faith, which for reasons that will gradually become more evident I would prefer to call *unitive faith,* is not a universal faith or religion as such. So let it remain a moot question, for the time being, whether any worldwide religion is possible. Instead, I will concentrate on what is meant *qualitatively* by a faith that would in some sense transcend the conjunctive stage.

We have already seen how conjunctive faith attempts to rise above the polarities of black and white, either/or thinking to achieve a dialectical synthesis that resolves all tensions. The problem is, however, that thinking is one thing and achieving is another. We have also seen how the constant awareness of both sides of any question can have the effect of mentally paralyzing a person to the extent that all committed action, indeed, commitment itself, ceases, and that what began with the appearance of conjunctive faith ends, at the worst, in a destructive cynicism, or, at best, in a sterile apathy.

This need not be the case. Indeed, enough persons of conjunctive faith live their lives, in a committed and active way, to provide much hope for the world and the human spirit. But is this enough?

The Perfection of Faith

As we have noted, some of Fowler's critics, even some friendly ones like Gabriel Moran (see Moran's 1983 *Religious Education Development*), have questioned whether such a "universalizing" faith exists, or, if it does, if it must be considered a goal for most persons. Admittedly, few do achieve it. Fowler's research interviews report to have turned up only one candidate, but that has not discouraged him from postulating that such a state exists and has been reached by a limited but significant number of examples in recent times—among them are two in particular who, in his estimation, have achieved this state and who I think best fit our needs of comparison and illustration in this consideration of the final stage of faith.

The Indian religious leader and social and political reformer Mohandas Gandhi (1869–1948) and the American monk and writer Thomas Merton (1915–1968) at first may seem to have little in common except the latter's admiration for the former. But we shall soon see there is much more that they had in common, not the least of which was a great ambition to achieve sanctity and to arrive at a universalizing or what I now describe as a unitive faith.

But the question remains as to how consistently these

two noted but controversial figures display all the earmarks of a truly mature faith. To answer that question, I think that there is no need to review the basic characteristics that such a faith would display. The key difference between it and a conjunctive faith, to my mind, would be the *resolution,* at least in terms of inward composure, of most, if not all of the contradictions or paradoxes that form the basis of the tensions that characterize conjunctive faith. Again, we also must be acutely aware that while such tensions can be theoretically resolved in one's head, the question of outward consistency often is something else.

Both Gandhi and Merton in some way transcended their origins by seeking inspiration from the opposite end of the world. Although he was raised as a Hindu, and greatly influenced by Jainism, the pacifist religion concentrated in his native district of India, Gandhi appears to have been even more strongly influenced by the Christian gospels and their radical interpretation by Count Leo Tolstoy, the Russian novelist and social reformer. Despite having only spent a few years in England as a student of the law, Gandhi's longer exposure to western ways during his years in South Africa steeled his determination to seek the truth wherever it is found, even when his return to his native India strengthened his resolve to remain a Hindu to the core.

Merton, on the other hand, was raised somewhat indifferently when it came to religious training—mostly in boarding schools in France and England. Still, after some brief exposure to Oriental religious thought, he turned to Catholicism as a young man, doing so almost with a vengeance, soon joining the strictest order of cloistered monks that the church provided. Isolated from the outside world, Merton only returned to his early interest in Oriental thought in the last few years of his relatively short life, drawn partly by its contemplative emphasis, and partly by his great concern for peacemaking and the example that Gandhi provided. But despite recurrent rumors, there can be no serious question that he also remained committed to his Christian faith and monastic vocation. So while both of these extraordinary men were, in the best sense, persons of truly ecumenical faith in the broadest sense of the word, yet each remained firmly rooted in the faith forms of his respective culture.

One thing else I think is striking. Although Gandhi and Merton became deeply committed to the moral transformation of society, both believed that the essential key to this change was *within*—that one could never expect to effectively influence society unless one's own self was radically transformed. In effect, both of these men early in their life consciously decided that their primary task, above all else, was to become a "saint." Both remained deeply suspicious of reformers who appear on the scene with radical programs but who, even with the best of intentions—or so they think —still have not been consistently transformed from within. In Gandhi's case this was evidenced by his decision to adopt the ascetical life, with all that entailed, even while he still remained a "householder," and particularly by his determination to live in the state of religious celibacy. Nor did Merton undertake his radical choice from a state of pure innocence or naiveté. Both knew that they possessed strong passions that demanded strong controls.

But the comparison between Gandhi and Merton should not stop there. Although both were men of keen intellect, neither had much patience for purely abstract thinking. Gandhi's determination, his "vow" even, to pursue the truth in a lived "experiment" was paralleled by Merton's own determination to withdraw from academic and literary society to live solely for God. Yet despite their high ideals, each in his own way had his feet of clay. Gandhi's rather harsh treatment of his wife and his virtual disowning of the son he hoped would follow in his footsteps, as well as his self-administered tests of his chastity, were cause for consternation. Merton's reappearing weakness for alcohol, along with the revelation of the love affair that he suffered through for some months about two years before his death, also came as something of a shock to those who knew and admired him (see Mott, *The Seven Mountains of Thomas Merton*).

What are we to think about such flaws or apparent inconsistencies in such exemplary men? Erik Erikson, from whom Fowler has taken much of his original inspiration, has this to say about Gandhi's often puzzling life:

> As to the Mahatma's *public private* life, all we can say is that here was a man who both lived and wondered aloud, and with equal intensity and depth, about a multiformity of inclinations which other men hide and bury in strenuous consistency. At the end *great confusion can be a mark of greatness,* too, especially if it results from the *inescapable conflicts of existence.* (Erikson, *Gandhi's Truth,* p. 405)

If this inconsistency seems baffling to find in a person like Gandhi, who sought to convert people by the example of his own life, it is no less so in Merton the writer, whose apostolate had become, to no small extent, bound up with the disclosure of his private self to his readership around the world.

Thus we find that the "final integration"—Erikson's last stage in his scheme of human maturation—does not always point to perfect harmony within. Nor does Jung's notion of "individuation" as involving a "coincidence of opposites" smack of tensionless existence. Although both Gandhi and Merton evidenced a truly universalizing or universalized faith vision and faith commitment, both to some extent failed to achieve the perfect harmony or integration that they sought. Ironically both ended up, not entirely by coincidence, coming closest to accomplishing this through what Erikson, in an earlier book, gave as representing the two extreme solutions of "the last problems"—martyrdom or solitude (see Erikson, *Young Man Luther*, 1958, p. 261). If Gandhi's assassination was hardly self-willed, still it culminated a whole life marked by what seemed at times to be an almost self-destructive urge to sacrifice self for others. And if Merton's almost constant battle to be allowed the solitude of the hermitage could be legitimately seen as a longing for what represents the purest form of the contemplative life, still the reappearing of what had seemed long-settled interior conflicts proves the truth of what the ancient desert fathers so often warned—that the call to solitude includes the call to confront the forces of evil head-on, and to discover that these forces lie deepest within one's self.

So a major part of the challenge of universalizing faith is to arrive at a stage of final integration. Neither are the major characteristics of this final stage of faith to be found in different beliefs or ideals, or even in higher ethical standards as compared to conjunctive faith, but rather, as Fowler points out, in terms of the *perspective* from which these are viewed or acted upon. Yet this new perspective is not simply one of a broadened world-view or horizon. Instead, a truly "universalizing" faith is most of all marked by a "*decentration from self.*" Thus one's perspective or horizon becomes not only detached from the limitations of class, ethnic, or even religious background, but takes on a cosmic dimension that strives to view all things from God's point of view. It is in that sense both a highly *contemplative* point of view, and, at the same time, one that demands the ultimate in *self-sacrifice* (see Fowler, 1985, pp. 68–70). It is for this same reason that Richard J. Sweeney, in his treatment of the subject, calls this final stage "sacrificial faith." And it is because of the immense difficulties involved in this self-transcending, yet self-fulfilling effort, the seeming contradiction of total integration of the self by forgetting self, that we must now confront these paradoxes directly.

The Risks of Sanctity

If I have concentrated on these two proffered instances of universalizing or unitive faith rather than tried to give a fuller clinical definition, it is because Gandhi and Merton, in their successes and failures, their consistencies and inconsistencies, illustrate both the challenge and the dangers of arriving at this goal better than any outline or list of qualities ever could. In the move from conjunctive to universalizing faith we see not so much any change in the description of faith as far as its abstract qualities are concerned, as instead we see more of a radical change in the person in question, a change that is hard to describe in any terms other than the difference between a good, even outstanding person and what, for want of a more globally all-inclusive term, we generally call a "saint."

But here I must also stress that a person can only *"arrive at"* sanctity rather than "achieve" sainthood. One can, to be sure, aim at becoming a saint. The question remains, however, whether this is possible through will-power alone. There can be no doubt that both Gandhi and Merton consciously set out to be nothing less than saints—yet each of them failed in rather glaring instances to fully achieve this goal. Nor should we be surprised, because this is where the paradox most of all lies, between intention and accomplishment. According to Christian doctrine, although we must *will* to cooperate, it is only through God, or the influence of *grace,* that this result can occur. Although I do not wish to get into the reformation controversy over the supposed difference between grace viewed as "justifying" (the more Protestant—especially, Lutheran—view, which seems to lie behind much of the sharper disagreement with Fowler's concept of "faith stages" to begin with) and grace as "sanctifying" (strongly defended by the Roman Church and by Fowler's own Methodist tradition). But there is more than just a little at stake here. Sainthood, according to the oldest tradition, is not just a matter of being "saved," as important as that may be. It is a matter of becoming "like God" or of *theosis* or "divinization"—to use the theological term of the Eastern Orthodox churches. Thus grace is seen not only as sanctifying but even as "deifying."

As Eric Fromm pointed out in his provocative study, *You Shall Be As Gods,* this is a most dangerous idea. Truly, God has created us to be like himself—"in his image and likeness" according to Genesis 1:26. But is not this that same ambition, that *hubris* or pride which in the Greek myths inevitably leads to the human downfall? Yes, so it is, yet in Fromm's point of view, it is not this goal that constitutes the core of human sinfulness—the *origin*-al nature of sin, if you will—but instead the self-deception involved in thinking that we can do so on our own terms. It is this underlying problem that explains some of Gandhi's and Merton's inconsistencies.

Granted that the ambition to become a saint is not an unworthy one, and that without a persistent quest for this goal few if any except a few of the more sudden martyrs will arrive at genuine sanctity. But again, desire is one thing, and accomplishment is another. According to Catholic-Orthodox theological tradition, some persons are "predestined" to achieve eminent sanctity, while others are not. So this amounts to saying that no matter how hard we may desire to become a "Saint," (here the capital "S" implying a publicly recognized or "canonized" one) it is still ultimately a question of God's will.

This means, more radically, that we must purify our ambitions in a way that, as Fowler says, "decentrates" our center of concern from ourselves and enables us to undergo a *kenosis* or "emptying out" in the biblical sense of the word. This is not a popular theme in an age dedicated to self-fulfillment—if indeed it ever was. Even in medieval times this pitfall in the quest of sanctity was recognized. Thus St. Bernard of Clairvaux's division of the life of contemplation into two stages: the first being our consideration of what is God's will *for us,* the second being what is God's will *in itself.* Or again, the reason for Meister Eckhart's emphasis on the necessity of *erlassen,* a "letting go," is the need to free ourselves not only from our worldly concerns but even from excessive concern for our own perfection.

This insistence on freedom from even the consuming *desire* for sanctity is quite easy to understand from the viewpoint of Frankl's basic dynamic. Sanctity or sainthood, viewed as a goal for ourselves to achieve, easily becomes another form of self-idolatry. It can become so in one or the other of two ways. We see it either as a goal to be sought for the *consolations* it will bring or else as a means of achieving *self-mastery* or *self-realization.*

Probably the first deviation, which is the Freudian pleasure principle in spiritual dress, appeals more to passive personalities, especially those drawn toward mysticism; for these, particularly, the lure of *security* in the form of feeling loved by God is the major risk. The second deviation, which amounts to the Adlerian goal translated into religious terms, is less security-motivated, but provides the perfect cover for the more power-oriented person who would see himself or herself as prophet-reformer, a spokesman or agent of God, a privileged calling that's made to order for the classical *causa sui* project—that of making oneself into one's own God.

It is for this reason that some philosophers and theologians have objected to the great patristic theme of *theosis* often expressed in the classical dictum about the incarnation: "God became man that man might become God." This theme, however, should not be taken literally but should always be modified in the scriptural sense of our intended "likeness" to God. But even that qualification aside, I think the key here is a question of emphasis. Irenaeus and those after him used this saying primarily to stress that in Jesus, God became totally *like us,* save in sin, in order that we might become as fully as possible like God. *Theosis,* in this scheme of reasoning, is totally subservient to, and reversely analogous to, the incarnation. Created in God's "image," we are called to live in the likeness of Christ, who "is the image of the invisible God" (Col 1:15). But granted the reality of the call "to be *perfected,* even as your heavenly Father is perfect" (Mt 5:48)—the key word here is *téleios,* meaning "perfect," "complete," "fulfilled," "mature"—the mere idea of sanctity, even a hidden sanctity, like the human desire for fulfillment, in itself has a subtle ability to corrupt the purest of human intentions. The *causa-sui* or "self-god" project, then, remains the final and most perilous of the deviations that are possible in the life of faith. It is the hidden trap that awaits those who would achieve the final stage of faith.

Fortunately for us, God's grace is not easily cheated. Those whom God has called are also given the means to avoid this or at least to overcome its grip. In the concrete, these preventive or corrective factors may differ greatly in their shape or form. But underneath they share a single, common denominator, one that at the root is directly connected with the central dynamism of the whole religious quest—the never-ending challenge for a continued growth and deepening of *faith.*

The Night of Faith

Alan Watts, the late religious philosopher of the hippie era, asserted that for the Oriental Christian tradition, there was no such thing as the so-called "dark night of faith." No doubt this phrase itself, and attention to the phenomenon to which it refers, only became widespread relatively late in the west. It was Watt's theory that this was because the eastern church tradition had always laid an equal stress on *apophatic* theology or the so-called *"via negativa"* as it had on *kataphatic* theology or the *"via positiva."* In the latter, the "positive" mode prevailing in the western tradition, we ascribe all the superlatives we can to God, then say that God is immeasurably greater than even that. In "negative" theology, on the other hand, we are content to say only what God *isn't* and concentrate on leaving more "space" in our minds, so to speak, for attempting to grasp what can never be adequately expressed.

The result has been that in the east the "creeds" were taken less literally and more symbolically from the beginning. Indeed, the Greek term for "creed" is *symballon*—literally, something that is "thrown together" as it were, by way of analogy. But in the west the prevailing tendency has been to turn to the "negative" mode of expression only out of desperation and through a process involving a near loss of faith in the sense of "beliefs." This process is so traumatic that it can be accurately described as a "dark night," according to the sixteenth century Spanish mystical writer John of the Cross (Juan de Yepes, 1542–1591).

Although Watt's diagnosis is an oversimplification, particularly as a judgment on more sophisticated western theological discourse, still when it comes to spirituality and piety, our human tendency is to hang on to the positive approach as long as we can. For whatever their insufficiencies, beliefs still give us a "handle" of some sort to which we can cling. Without the security afforded by our beliefs or faith convictions, we fear suffering psychological and theological vertigo. This is understandable enough, but should we put off this confrontation with the limits of human thought to the very last moment as we generally do? Is this wise theologically, or even pedagogically? How many persons have been lost to Christianity when no alternative was offered them after they began to see the manifest inadequacies, not just of symbolic phrases like "seated at the right hand of God," or "heaven above," or the like, but also of the analogical use of terms such as "person," and "nature" as applied within theological constructs?

There is more at stake here than just mental confusion. There is the whole matter of the core dynamism of faith as such. If *convictions* are a necessary part of faith, still convictions that are too readily expressed in symbolic terms easily run the risk of becoming idols with all the bigotry, self-delusion, and other related dangers we have seen associated with such an objectification of the transcendent dimension of reality. When this happens, the *commitment* itself tends to become distorted. Too often the apparent *security* offered by the creeds, for all practical purposes, has taken the place of God.

Is there a way around this trap? I believe there is—but Christian readers will have to be patient with me, for to best understand it would be helpful to take a serious look at Oriental religious thought, and particularly those forms of Buddhism which so fascinated Merton—much to the consternation of some of his Christian readership. I suggest this because, to my mind, this ancient tradition addresses this problem more directly and thoroughly, even if, to western eyes, too extremely, than any other religious and philosophical tradition.

Historically, all that we know for sure about the fabled sixth century B.C. Indian prince Siddartha Gautama, now known as "the Buddha" or "the enlightened one," is that, after searching for *the* meaning of life, of suffering, and of divinity, he had come to the conclusion that the various religious doctrines and most of the ascetic practices of classical Hinduism not only fail to bring enlightenment but only serve to prevent us from truly experiencing ultimate reality. Instead Gautama sat down under a tree near Banares and vowed not to rise until he found the answer. What that answer was is contained under the "four noble truths" and "the eightfold path," none of which say anything about the nature of ultimate reality, but instead attempt to tell us how to reach that reality. The four truths are simply:

- To live is to suffer.
- The cause of suffering is desire.

- This desiring can be overcome.
- The way to do this is to live according to the eightfold path.

The eightfold path, in turn, is first of all a mental-volitional discipline of "right thinking" or correct ideas, and "right aim," secondly, an ethical discipline of "right speech," "right action" and "right occupation," and, finally, a spiritual regimen consisting of "right effort," "right mindfulness" or attentiveness, and "right concentration" or meditation. This program, which Gautama and his disciples considered a "middle way" of tempered asceticism, was structured within a monastic life lived in simplicity, poverty and celibacy. *Theraveda* or "The Way of the Elders" (sometimes called *Hinayana* or the "Lesser Vehicle") Buddhism in Southeast Asia still stresses this original and largely monastic form. *Mahayana,* or the "Greater Vehicle" Buddhism that predominates in the rest of the far east, is much more adapted to full lay participation. Despite some deep doctrinal differences, particularly regarding the attitude taken toward the Buddha himself—for the Theravedins he is a saint, but, for Mahayanists, an incarnation of the Divine itself—what both major groups as well as all their many subdivisions have to a large extent in common is a generally "apophatic" or negative approach to ultimate reality. In contrast to that theologically developed Hinduism which speaks of the *Atman* as the higher, imperishable spirit at the depth of our existence and its identity with *Brahman* or the divine essence, Buddhism contrasts the doctrine of *anatta* or "selflessness" (*an-atman* or "no-soul") where the transient self reaches enlightenment in the form of *nirvana* or *nibbana*—which literally means a "blowing out" or "extinguishing" (as of a lamp or candle), or as it were, in a sense, "annihilation" within the formless, infinite void.

Westerners, when they first begin to understand Buddhist thought, are often shocked, for there is no clearly identified personal "God" in Buddhism; indeed, except in some popular Mahayanist sects, the use of the terms "God" or "gods" is generally avoided, so that in a certain sense Buddhism is "atheistic." But it would be more accurate to say that Buddhism is characterized by a reverent agnosticism. Thus in its substitute term for the ultimate, *nirvana,* according to most Buddhists, the "blowing out" or "extinguishing" is not to be taken literally but as symbolic of the ultimate reality that can be approached only through total self-forgetfulness which at the same time will bring us to total enlightenment and self-realization.

However, as we shall see, the main point is that to reach this state, one must resolutely reject all attempts to define it. To try to define or describe the ultimate self, the ultimate state, or the divine ultimate, or to even say for sure that they exist, is to endanger the whole process in a fruitless effort of trying to avoid the absolute necessity of unconditional and unsupported faith or trust.

The reason I have gone into this whole matter of Buddhism, trying to simplify a very complicated matter, is because I think it is essential to follow the logic of this thinking when it comes to understanding the "decentration" of self demanded by a truly universalizing or fully unitive faith. The Buddhist approach may seem extreme, but, psychologically speaking, I don't think it is necessarily any more so than the teaching of St. John of the Cross. It is striking that this sixteenth century Spaniard's most famous set of maxims summing up his doctrine also exhibits an almost Buddhist-like avoidance of the all-too-familiar use of the word "God." Instead we find:

> To reach satisfaction in all,
>   desire its possession in nothing.
> To come to possess all,
>   desire the possession of nothing.
> To arrive at being all,

desire to be nothing.
To come to the knowledge of all,
    desire the knowledge of nothing . . .

and

To come to the knowledge you have not,
    you must go by a way you know not.
To come to the possession you have not,
    you must go by a way in which you possess not.
To come to be what you are not,
    you must go by a way in which you are not.
                    (*The Ascent of Mt. Carmel,*
                        Book I, Chap. 13.11)

Admittedly there is much argument about these verses
—which I have abbreviated somewhat. But I've certainly
given enough to convey their shocking emphasis on the
apophatic way of negation, which is even more evident in
the original Spanish, with its frequent use of the double
negative (*"no quieras . . . nada"*)—this in contrast to the
overwhelming totality of the divine "all" (*todo*). Although
the double negatives should be normally translated as a single negative in English, the problem is how, and with what
emphasis; for example, are we being advised "to desire to
know *nothing*" or "to *not* desire to know anything" (or literally, "anything in [about?] nothing")?

This may seem like academic quibbling, but the key
problem here, as I see it, just as in the Buddha's "four noble
truths" is the question of *desire*. The word *tanha* in the Pali
dialect that Gautama spoke meant simply that. But as the
revered Zen philosopher, D.T. Suzuki, insisted, this hardly
makes sense when taken literally. Without the desire to be
enlightened and to escape pointless suffering, a person
would hardly bother to try to follow the Buddha's way. So
most commentators believe that Gautama was talking only

about *selfish* or egocentric desire, often translated as "craving." But on the other hand, the Buddhist doctrine of *anatta* or "no-self" seems to indicate that it is more than the simple (but never easy) matter of purifying one's desires. Rather, as we shall see, it is the very concept of "self" that seems suspect.

In John of the Cross, however, the paradox is even more consciously emphasized. To begin with, he appears to have no hesitation in exploiting the power of human desire, seeing it as a God-given life impulse, particularly when turned toward the goal of self-fulfillment. But just as surely he then turns around and seems to stress the negation of this same desire. But again, if we see this simply as an attempt to purify desire rather than diminish it, why then the jarring use of the double negative? We are told not just to avoid desiring what is relatively "nothing," but really to let go of desiring as such. Why? Because the more *we* try to eliminate *our* selfishness, our *self* keeps getting in the way, and all the more so the harder we try.

Probably this is the best explanation of why in many, if not all, Buddhist philosophies, the doctrine of *anatta* is taken with great metaphysical, and not just psychological seriousness; the living, thinking *self* is considered to be an *illusion,* the result of a mere conglomeration of bodily functions, thoughts, and cravings. For once you have eliminated the belief that you really exist, then you have undercut the tap root of all selfishness. Christianity, of course, cannot go this far. Like the Hindus, Christians generally believe in an indestructible, immortal self or *soul.* Hence the problem faced by John of the Cross and other Christian thinkers: how best purify the self from selfishness without reinforcing self-consciousness and self-concern, and, with it, self-centeredness?

But there is one other possible interpretation of the Buddhist approach to this perennial problem. It is to be found in one of the major Mahayanist schools known as

Madhyamika or "Middle Path" Buddhism—not to be confused with Gautama's own claim that his was a "middle
way" of moderated asceticism. Founded by the Indian
teacher Nagarjuna around the beginning of the third century
of our era, it employs an elaborate dialectic to psychologically break down any reliance on doctrines, particularly regarding such matters as the immortality of the soul, the per-
manence of the world, and the nature of the ultimate.
Nagarjuna resolutely refused to allow for intellectual solutions to these questions, apparently seeing them as the greatest barrier to direct intuitive experience. This whole approach, which I suspect probably comes closest to
recapturing the original intent of Gautama's teaching, has
obviously also had a strong influence, along with the Chi-
nese philosophy of the *Tao,* on Zen Buddhist thought.

Now if we transpose this last approach from Madhyamika Buddhism to the doctrine of John of the Cross, what do
we have? I think, if I am right, that we suddenly arrive at an
insight into why the final dark night in John's description of
the spiritual ascent is a night of *faith*—that is, a darkening or
obscuring of all the sureness or security given by religious
doctrines or dogma. Such doctrines are meant to be nothing
more than pointers toward the divine. But once they are
taken too seriously or too literally, they become idols which
obscure the divine. And the transposition from this understanding of Buddhism to Christianity works both ways. It is
significant that Suzuki told Merton, much to his surprise,
that Merton's early book, *The Ascent to Truth*—a book Merton very much disliked—was read with much appreciation
by Japanese Zen students who considered its exposition of
the basic doctrine of John of the Cross as an exemplary
western insight into Zen—this despite Merton's uncompli-
mentary remarks about Oriental mysticism at the time.

So what are we to think about these austere doctrines,
whether in their Buddhist or in their Christian form? Per-

haps it is not every Buddhist's cup of tea, and even John of the Cross admitted that what he wrote was not necessarily offered to everyone but rather to those who wished to advance more quickly. But I wonder if, in the end, we can escape it. Lay Buddhists—and, I suppose, tired monks—are tempted to hope it can be put off until another life. Catholics conclude that the final stripping of self shall, in most cases, have to wait for purgatory. Both sentiments are probably quite realistic in terms of what most of us hope to achieve in this life. Yet the gospels seem to challenge us to much more than this. To those who wonder what advantages faith provides them in this life, Jesus urges us "to seek first the kingdom of God, and then everything else will be given to you besides" (Mt 6:33). For those who seek immortality: "He who seeks to save his life will lose it, and he who loses his life for my sake will save it" (Lk 17:33). It seems there really is no escape from this inexorable law. It is not some exclusive principle of spiritual growth that we are dealing with, but instead what is a fundamental and universal law of nature: "Unless a grain of wheat falls into the earth and dies, it cannot bear fruit . . ." (Jn 12:24). Is there any reason to think that the life of faith itself is an exception?

Here I'm reminded of the story about St. Thérèse of Lisieux, a young Carmelite nun who died of tuberculosis in 1897. It is related that in the months just before her death the other sisters, in an effort to cheer her up, would exclaim to her how wonderful it must be to know that she would soon be in heaven with God and the saints. Her answer was on occasion most disconcerting—when she tried to think of such things, she confessed, she was assailed by doubts whether heaven or even God exists! Or as Watts put it: "The incredible truth [is] that what religion calls the vision of God is found in giving up any belief in the *idea* of God." (See Watts, *The Wisdom of Insecurity,* p. 27—emphasis mine.) Our ideas, our beliefs, are too often our idols.

Faith Beyond Beliefs

What then? Does the final stage of faith lead to nihilism, to loss of faith? Often it may seem so at the time. The "dark night" can be an extremely frightening thing. There are many ways that these nights of faith can come upon a person, not all of them intellectual. The suffering of difficulties of one type or another, sometimes as a result of family and occupational problems, losses by death, the onset of illness, or simply even the caprices of mood swings—all these can be the occasion of a "night" in the broad sense of a period of trial that often turns out to be the catalyst of interior transformation. Consider this following account supplied to me by a correspondent who had been going through a prolonged period of physical exhaustion, psychological depression, and doubts about his faith.

> To get away I had gone fishing but had fallen asleep alongside a stream. Instead of waking up refreshed, I awoke with a great sense of oppression bearing down on me. Then all of a sudden—I can't explain it—I seemed to be lifted up, not physically, or anything like that, but it was like I was being cradled in someone's arms, but not those of a tangible or visible person, but by an engulfing, loving presence. At that point time seemed suspended and I realized that alive or dead, it is all the same. I was given to know that we all exist as part of a vast totality within which our puny individual existence means little in itself and yet is infinitely precious in the eyes of this loving being. After what seemed an hour, but may have only been a few minutes, I got up, walked back to my car and drove to a friend's cabin where I tried to write an account of what had happened. But all descriptions eluded me. I only knew that in some way I no longer had to merely "believe" that God exists—I had experienced God first-hand!

Undoubtedly this account reflects what Abraham Maslow called a "peak-experience," in Maslow's estimation not an unusual occurrence for many persons. Such experiences seem to manifest a distinctively *mystical* dimension—if we mean by "mysticism" that in such events in some way one encounters the ultimate ground of our existence or experiences a sense of unity with the divine.

No doubt, the attempt to express what this unity is, and the person or power with which one feels united, varies vastly according to one's cultural or theological background. The Oriental religions seem to stress the notion of identity or total absorption of the individual in the divine or the ultimate. Western religion, with its strong sense of the divine "otherness" or transcendence of God, more typically expresses such a relationship in terms of "vision" or person-to-person encounter. But the overall pattern is unmistakable; it is an overwhelming conviction of creaturely *union* with the divine—hence my preference for the term "unitive faith."

I am struck by one other thing, and that is the similarity of the effects of such distinctively theological or mystical "peak-experiences" to the so-called "near-death experiences." This is not in the more commonly reported visual representations, such as viewing one's own body as it were from above, the passage through a "tunnel," the approach of an overwhelming light, and so on, but in the specifically religious effect that such experiences seem to have in common with the unitive type of mystical peak-experience.

Dr. Raymond Moody, the main compiler of near-death experience data, recounts in his most recent book *The Light Beyond* that typically persons who have had such experiences, whether previously religious or not, inevitably seem to undergo a "conversion" that results in a markedly deepened dedication to their own spiritual growth and their relatedness to God or the pursuit of ultimate meaning in life. But even more striking is his observation that overtly religious people, those who have been long affiliated with a particular church or faith, almost to a person report that their previous faith has become relativized—or should we say universalized?—at least in the sense that they are now convinced that their particular faith formulas or convictions are now seen to be more or less inadequate, and to some degree no longer necessary.

This last point interests me greatly. The relativization of faith statements, which are patently symbolic in nature, is one thing. In some sense we have arrived at a state of faith *beyond* reliance on any particular beliefs. But are we here being told that to some extent the person has passed beyond the necessity for faith itself?

In some ways this appears to be the case, especially when faith is taken to be a set of convictions or beliefs accepted on the *authority* of others. The person quoted above said that after his experience, he felt that never again would he have to "believe" in God—that now he "knew" first-hand that God exists. Probably it is more accurate to say that, in the first place, belief in the existence of God is not so much a belief at all but more like the result of logical reasoning. So for many persons, the real issue is not whether this "first cause" or "ground of being" exists, but whether it exists as a loving, caring "father"-like or "mother"-like "person." What happens in such unitive experiences as we have described is that these persons no longer have to be convinced, by logical arguments, that God is this loving, all-encompassing entity, or, on the other hand, simply trust that is so. Instead, they have had, they are convinced, an actual experience of such a God or divine presence and ultimate meaning.

Does such an experience eliminate the necessity of faith? Not certainly in the sense of *commitment*—on the contrary, the typical result of such unitive experience is deepened commitment. But again, according to Moody, part of this commitment is to learn more (even academically— many recovered "near-death" subjects reenroll in school) and to search ever more assiduously for a total integration of their lives in service of humanity and continued experiences of the divine.

But most of all, what we see is a profoundly grounded sense of *confidence,* especially among those who have had this experience in a near-death context. They simply no longer fear death any more—indeed one of the more common hallmarks of the experience is a sense of their either having been given a choice to "come back" to life in this world or to stay on the "other side" or else having been told that they couldn't stay but had to return, no matter how reluctantly, to this world to accomplish the rest of God's will for their lives. Many who claim mystical experiences report much the same. Recall the gospel accounts of Jesus' "transfiguration" where Peter wanted to set up "three shelters" for the principals in the vision: Christ, Moses, and Elijah; instead the apostles are brusquely brought back to normal consciousness (see especially Mk 9:1–7).

Does all this mean that a person who has had such an experience will never have a doubt again or waver in his or her commitment, or ever suffer any fear or loss of confidence? Again, if the subsequent history of Peter and the other apostles as pictured in the New Testament is any indication, such a total transformation is hardly guaranteed. A momentary unitive experience does not guarantee sanctity by any means. But in the long run it is a help or incentive in that direction. Few people honored as saints today seem to have been without one or two such experiences during their lives, while a lucky few seemed to live in an almost constant state of union with God.

Maslow, in his new introduction in a later edition to his now-classic *Religions, Values, and Peak-Experiences,* made several important additions or corrections to his earlier observations. Maslow wrote that in addition to an expanded view of peak-experiences that would include near-death and other "nadir" experiences, he also must take careful note of

so-called "plateau-experience" as described by such researchers as R. Johnson or the "easy state" of Asrani, which
is "serene and calm . . . [having] a poetic and cognitive element . . . far more voluntary than peak experiences are. One
can learn to see in this *Unitive* way almost at will" (emphasis
mine). Furthermore, Maslow went on to say:

> . . . plateau experience can be achieved, learned,
> earned by long hard work. It can be meaningfully
> aspired to. But I don't know of any bypassing of the
> necessary maturing, experiencing, living, learning.
> All of this takes time. A transient glimpse is cer-
> tainly possible in the peak experiences which may,
> after all, come sometimes to anyone. But so to
> speak, to take up residence on the high plateau of
> Unitive consciousness, that is another matter alto-
> gether. (As quoted by Margaret Gorman, *Psychol-
> ogy and Religion*, p. 306)

Contrasted to the momentary "grace" of a peak-experience, Maslow stressed the great effort necessary to achieve
this "plateau" of higher consciousness. Although some of
the saints and mystics seem to have been gifted from the
start with this more permanent sense of union with God, still
this grace or gift more generally seems to have come only
after a long period of purification, both self-administered as
well as by trials permitted by God. But there also seems to be
no question that, even apart from sainthood, such unitive
consciousness can be to some extent achieved by dint of
hard work. Yet there can be no sure-fire techniques, magic
formulas or psychedelic short-cuts to *genuine* unitive consciousness.

Yet if there has been widespread confusion over this
matter, perhaps this only serves to underline the difference
between higher states of consciousness and sanctity as such.
It is hard to imagine sanctity existing without this conscious-

ness and the effort that it takes—sanctity being, to my mind, a conscious and consistent effort to live out the full implications of such a unitive state. No doubt there have been real saints whose faith in some ways fell somewhat short of this unitive and universalizing level, but I would suspect that now, in the light of eternity, their vision has become expanded. So while the ability to live on a "plateau" level of unitive consciousness does not necessarily translate into sanctity, or vice versa, still without such an expanded vision or the effort to achieve it, I doubt few saints are made.

All this raises another question: saints or not, do such persons of unitive faith tend to become alienated in any way from ordinary religiosity and belief? Maslow also admitted that his earlier view was too one-sided in its individualism at the expense of "groups, organizations, and communities"— in other words, in following Jung who claimed that such experiences were essentially "outside the church" (*"extra ecclesiam"*). But occasionally we see examples of where such apparent alienation has taken place—for example, we are told of one of the famed early "desert fathers" who lived on the Egyptian-Palestinian frontier. He could only be persuaded with the greatest reluctance to leave his hermitage to even make one pilgrimage to the holy places in and around Jerusalem. He finally did so, it seems, more out of fear of causing scandal than any wish to see the revered shrines. But on the whole what I think we see more often is an ability to see mystically *through* belief and custom to the essence of things. Yet occasionally the effects of such experiences are devastating. We can see this in the story of the most famous of the medieval theologians, St. Thomas Aquinas. After a great mystical experience toward the end of his life he is said to have refused to dictate another word and to have told his secretary, Brother Reginald, that compared to what he had experienced, all that he had written was as so much "straw."

If this is the case, what then of doctrine, ritual, and the other externals of religion? Does it all become, to some extent, "relativized"—or, to put a more positive term in its place, "universalized"? Perhaps so, in the sense that while one remains rooted in one's own tradition, at the same time the doors and windows are opened to take in whatever one finds of value in the traditions of others. Here one finds oneself drawn increasingly beyond the limitations of one's own faith and constantly looks for a higher synthesis, which, even if it can't be articulated, one is certain that it exists. Thus a unitive faith to some degree is almost always bound to be universalizing in its effect on a person's horizons—both on one's intellectual outlook and the scope of one's love.

Conclusion

We have seen, then, that this final "unitive" stage of faith not only tends to relativize "beliefs" but to some extent, in its breakthrough to religious experience, it appears even to minimize the need for faith itself—at least in any sense but renewed commitment to living out what one has to some degree already experienced. But this seeming transcendence of faith is only apparent. Not just reliance on "beliefs" but our faith commitment itself will be severely tested. But how?

Despite what Maslow had to say about the discipline required to attain "plateau experience," or what the saints taught about the desirability of this state of conscious union with God as an incentive toward a life of holiness, neither this experience nor more occasional "peak experiences" can be safely willed as ends or goals in themselves. Like sanctity itself, such experiences must remain subservient and secondary to the quest for God and the accomplishment of God's will. The security or consolation that such experiences represent can just as easily become a trap that frustrates any genuine development or progress in spirituality as can any attachment to a lesser good. Just as a deliberate courting of "near-death" experiences could be disastrous to one's physical health, the desire for mystical states or an active quest for ecstatic experience could prove fatal to one's spiritual growth.

John of the Cross is relentless in his doctrine of the way of faith; complete renunciation of all egocentric quests for consolation cannot be escaped. For as he wrote:

> When you turn toward something
> you cease to cast yourself upon the all.
> For to go from all to the all
> you must deny yourself of all in all.
> (*The Ascent of Mt. Carmel,* I.13.11)

The quest for mystical or ecstatic experience *for its own sake* is the hallmark of a false and self-centered mysticism, the quest to "have it all" for oneself apart from the divine will. This is true just as much as—or even more than—the employment of such self-delusionary agents as hallucinogenic drugs or other questionable means. As dangerous as these false paths to ecstasy are, the self-intoxication or the narcissism they merely represent remains the most insidious drug of all. Even genuine religious experience, when it is pursued for its own sake, will prove an obstacle to growth. The role of the "dark night" of faith is not just to purify us from over-reliance on beliefs and other symbolic props. God will see to it that "dark nights" will recur whenever we attempt to substitute anything, even the authentic experience of the divine, in place of the pure reliance on God in faith alone.

Thus we must conclude, when all is said and done, that *faith,* informed and energized by love, remains, in one form or another, the foundation and mainstay of all spiritual growth or development. Love may well outweigh faith in merit, and in the end supplant it, while hope points toward its fulfillment. But in this life there is simply no way around it. What else can a fully human life be in this insecure world but a life lived in the risk of faith?

Questions for Reflection and Discussion

1. Can you think of any other candidates for an outstanding example of a "universalizing" or unitive faith?
2. Give an example (preferably from your own life) where the attempt to be perfect resulted in just the opposite. What was your reaction to this discovery?
3. How explain or justify religion's appeal to selfish motives like "saving one's soul" or escape from suffering? How can (or should) religion try to rise above this?
4. Can you recall (and possibly share) your memories of a "peak experience" that you feel was, in some sense, a personal encounter with God? To what extent should such experiences (or the level of "plateau experience") be pursued? Why or why not?

Epilogue: Can There Be
a Universal Faith?

After our discussion of any "unitive" or so-called "universalizing" faith, this problem simply cannot be avoided. To the extent that unitive consciousness tends to universalize faith, the question of a *universal* faith or set of beliefs naturally follows; consequently not only every known major religious faith but even most of the great mystics themselves have made the claim of their own special insight into ultimate reality and, on the basis of that claim, tended to absolutize their own views as the superior, sometimes the only way, of approaching God or achieving salvation. Thus the subjective experience of unity with the absolute all too easily becomes the exclusive claim to absolute objectivity. The truth as grasped by this or that person or culture is elevated to the status of the sole ultimate truth for all persons, all cultures.

Theologian Hans Küng, in his book *Theology for the Third Millennium,* sums up the possible alternative reactions to this claim of religious faith. They are basically four (with Küng's phrasing given in italics):

1. *No religion is true* Or *all religions are equally untrue—*this usually meant in the sense of absolute atheism.
2. *Only one religion is true* Or *all other religions are untrue*—this is the "absolutist-exclusivist" position.
3. *Every religion is true* Or *all religions are equally true—*this is seen as a typically "relativistic" approach.
4. *Only one religion is* (essentially) *true* [while] *all other religions have a share* ([more or less]) *in the truth of this one religion*—generally termed the "inclusivist" view.

In light of the various faith stages, we have to eliminate the first two choices given above. Both dogmatically preclude any further discussion, neither qualifying for consideration by either a truly conjunctive or a universalizing faith. The first, "absolute atheism," reflects, as it usually does, the extreme negative or rejecting phase of the process that would otherwise lead toward a personal faith. Rather than being a cautious agnosticism, such a dogmatic rejection of all religion often assumes all the trappings and intolerance of a competing religion—for example, as seen in the official atheistic propaganda of the communist world.

Much the same degree of fanaticism mars the second possible response, the "absolute-exclusivist" position. This attitude, which often accompanies literal and conventional faith, unfortunately sometimes displays even more intolerance when it is taken into a more personal faith. Long the stance of most of the Christian denominations—either regarding themselves or Christianity as a whole—this second position was essentially repudiated by the Catholic Church at Vatican II.

The third possibility, however, is especially appealing to the conjunctive and unitive stages of faith, despite its questionable logic. It is claimed, for example, that each religion, within its cultural setting, essentially performs the same function—giving ultimate meaning to life. Some will go further and claim that all the religions have the same essential message. But I would dispute both claims. No doubt *any* religion gives some meaning to life. But are *all* meanings of equal value? For example, can a faith that turns its back entirely on the world be considered functionally the equal of one that tries to transform the world? Or, on the other hand, can we say that a religion that promises worldly success be considered as advanced as one that seeks to develop higher consciousness of and unity with the ultimate truth? Obviously, even by the criteria we've seen developed in our consideration of the stages of faith, there are serious gaps and contradictions in a purely relativist view of this type.

So this leaves us with the fourth possibility, what would be an "inclusivist" and, I presume, universalized view—but the problem here is: of *which* "true" religion? Küng points out that this is essentially the view taken by Hinduism as it has evolved in recent times, while we might add that Christian theologians, including Küng, are scrambling to come up with a convincing Christian version of the same. Even just a sketchy review of what has been attempted along this line so far would require another whole book.

This is the reason that I decided to avoid, as much as I could, up till now, the term "universalizing" faith or, even more, the suggestion of a "universal faith." Not that I don't believe that one is theoretically possible—it is just that the importance of faith understood primarily as *commitment,* and only secondarily as a set of convictions leading to an all-enabling confidence or trust, has been the main point, even if not the whole point of this book.

Yet the fact is that strong commitment cannot be made, except to someone or something. And, accordingly, certain *convictions* about that object of our commitment come to the fore. Unfortunately, even error, when firmly held, can sometimes inspire the highest confidence. Given the wrong set of convictions, that same confidence can wreak havoc upon the human mind and upon the world. Ultimately, only "the truth will make you free."

Truth involves, whether we like it or not, teachings or doctrine. But doctrines unfortunately still tend to divide more than unite. This is why Hinduism's and especially Buddhism's attempts to solve the problem propose to side-step the issue of doctrine altogether by relegating it to a lesser level of religious consciousness—of course, by advocating a "higher" mystical doctrine of their own. Or else one may attempt a synthesis of competing doctrines—such was the idea of the founder of Sikhism who attempted to blend the Hindu world-view, with its belief in *karma* and reincarnation, with Islamic monotheism. Unfortunately, history shows that such attempts at syncretism often turn out to become just another competing sect.

So too in the west. Not even the attempt to formulate a universalized interpretation of Christianity has ever been very successful, with what one group or another considers "heresy" dividing such efforts almost from the beginning. So also many groups stubbornly resist the ecumenical movement today. Nor has organized ecumenism's strategic shift to "service" instead of doctrine been noticeably more effective—in fact many of the moral and political dimensions of such service turn out to be more divisive than pure doctrine alone.

What then is the answer? Does the unitive faith stage inevitably call for not just a universalizing, but a truly *universal* faith? I am personally convinced that despite the divisive effect religious teachings have had in the past, only a deepened religious *faith* in the broadest sense of the word—which includes doctrine—can generate the hope, confidence, or trust that makes life possible in the long run. So I would like to end with a short consideration of what the content or convictions of that faith might include, at least from a Christian perspective. It is not the only and hardly the latest such attempt, but it is the one with which I am most familiar, and because of its emphasis on *faith* both as a *conviction* leading to *confidence* or hope for this world, as well as to a renewed *commitment* to the future of humanity, it is most appropriate for concluding our discussion.

About seventy years ago, the scientist-philosopher-theologian Pierre Teilhard de Chardin (1881–1955) began pondering the question of humanity's future in the face of a growing pessimism. We have, he felt, reached an impasse in the evolution of the human species; either we shall have to make the difficult choices that are necessary to advance, or else we will slowly, but surely, regress (see "The Grand Option" in *The Future of Man*). And that choice, he said, is essentially a question of *faith*, a faith that must combine both a "propulsive" faith in the future of humanity along the horizontal horizon of this world's evolution, as well as an "ascensional" faith that aims at the transcendental goal of the spirit (see "How I Believe" in *Christianity and Evolution*). To Teilhard's mind, the classical faiths or religions of mankind had fallen into a trap: either the development of the "soul" or spirit at the expense of this world, or else, as in the case of western and Marxist civilization, development of this world at the expense of the spirit. These two "faiths" must be reunited, and the world must search for *the* religious expression that is capable of doing so. For Teilhard, as a Christian, the symbolic goal of this dual faith is the "Christ-Omega," the focal point in which creator and creation are brought into a union through which "God becomes all in all" (1 Cor 15:28).

If I were to attempt to recast Teilhard's vision in trinitarian terms (or should we say Hegelian terms?—something similar to R. Panikkar's venture some years back) we might say that what Teilhard attempted to do was to reach a synthesis of the western emphasis on the transcendent "Father" God-image, on the one hand, and the immanential tendency of Oriental religion on the other. The latter's tendency to immerse divinity within the universe as its "soul" or "spirit," which, to Teilhard's mind, paradoxically tends to devaluate the material, changing universe as *maya* or illusion, too often ends up cultivating an indifference to the world as something not really real. Teilhard's approach to a synthesis of the two is based on a progressive or evolutionary view of the universe where "spirit" is not opposed to "matter," but where the two are seen but as poles of a single *weltstoff* and what appears to be pure materiality evolves, through a process of complexity leading toward consciousness, into what is more and more capable of full communion with God in love.

The great agent of this evolution is God's "Word" or the self-manifestation of God in human form, Jesus Christ. In him are not only the two views of divinity, transcendence and immanence of God, united, but through the evolution of his own humanity into a perfect instrument of the spirit, Jesus himself becomes the concrete embodiment of the "Omega"-goal of evolution where materiality itself is transformed into the consummate expression of the spirit. Yet, at the same time, the risen Christ is physically united to the universe, not just as the ecclesial or even the sacramental "body of Christ," but through him the universe itself becomes, as it were, "the body of God" or the *pleroma,* "the fullness of him who is filled all in all," or, as some translations put it, "who fills the universe in all its parts" (see Eph 1:23).

Teilhard himself never developed an express "pneumatology" or theology of the Holy Spirit, but his writings are pregnant with possibilities. His concept of the "noosphere," the interconnected "skein" or network of consciousnesses pushed ever more tightly together by "planetary compression" (the effect of ever-expanding population on a limited earth surface), not only portends a growing "world-culture" (as well as a world population crisis unless astutely managed) but also a growing unanimity of spiritual aspirations —even perhaps a drawing together of the world's religions. We can no longer ignore the existence of and the values of the other religious traditions. Either we learn to draw together under the attraction of that great spiritual pole and through the force of its primary energy, love, or else we will implode upon ourselves in an orgy of disharmony and self-destructive friction. Just as Christ's "body" grows, so to speak, through its expression in Christianity (or to Teilhard's mind, in whatever is "christified" in creation), so, too, cannot we say that God's Holy Spirit "grows" as it were, where and whenever the spiritual potentialities of the universe are developed and unified (or, as Teilhard would say, "amorized") through the power of love?

No doubt such a vision, however philosophically astute in speculative terms, is neither scientifically well-founded according to the methodology of biological science nor even theologically well-grounded according to the canons of biblical scholarship. At best, it resembles, somewhat vaguely, the Christology begun in the later Pauline "captivity" epistles (Colossians and Ephesians). The historical figure of Jesus presented in the scriptures, (especially the first three "synoptic" gospels) becomes all but swallowed up in the suprahistorical personage of the "universal Christ"—the universal meeting point between God and humanity.

In addition, in the face of the claims of the other major world religions, Jesus of Nazareth becomes (to Teilhard's mind, expressed in a later unpublished "Journal" note) the "definitive" (but, it seems, not the exclusive) manifestation of the "Trans-Christ"—the revelation of the divine "Logos" within the universe, which, by implication, has expressed itself in manifest ways, perhaps even in other "incarnations."

What are we to think of such speculations? No one can doubt the daring power of his thought—Teilhard even seriously pondered the implications of not just the possibility but even the virtual certainty of life on other planets. But, as Küng (1988) implies, not only do such flights of theological fancy break with the claims of the gospel as the absolute norm (the "*norma normans*") for Christian theology, but Teilhard's naive belief in the "infallibility" of human evolution, which so scandalized his Roman censors, is, in our "post-modern" period, a passé remnant of a bygone era. We can no longer be so optimistic about this world or our abilities to shape its future. So are we not dealing here with a mystical vision of sorts, a personal faith of one extraordinary individual that just happened to fill the needs of many persons seeking a new faith or a new sense of security in a very insecure time? Perhaps. No doubt there is much truth in these criticisms.

Nevertheless, I believe there is also something more to be said in his favor. Teilhard's synthesis, because of its mystical dimension, represents for me the clearest example of a conjunctive faith straining toward a unitive resolution—for what could be, at first glance, more paradoxically disjunctive than a faith in *both* the "infallibility" of the world *and* in the God of biblical tradition who "thinks, loves, speaks, punishes, rewards in the same way as a *person* does"? (See *Christianity and Evolution,* p. 99.) How expand trust in Jesus of Nazareth into a faith in the universal Christ except as the product of a *unitive* vision that embraces, all at once, God and cosmos, the "pantheistic" insights of the east and the "personalistic" views of the west? (See "The Spiritual Contribution of the Far East" and "The Road of the West" in *Toward the Future.*) This necessity for a new, expanded faith is at once the driving force, the underlying motif, and as often as not the featured theme of a whole lifetime's worth of his writings.

If I have brought this discussion to a close by turning to Teilhard's version of "The Evolution of Faith" (the introductory section of "How I Believe") it is not because I think his is the only possible version of a unitive vision that reaches out toward a universal faith. There have been and will be many more such attempts—Teilhard perhaps only having been one of those *"precursors"* (see Küng, 1988, pp. 186 and 214) who attempted to speculatively bridge the gap between traditional belief and modern scientific views. But I personally think that it was less a matter of Teilhard's speculative genius and more the power of his unitive consciousness that inspired him in his universalizing synthesis and his attempts to formulate a universal faith. For Teilhard, "research" was the cutting edge of evolution, and mysticism the highest form of research.

Teilhard more than once remarked in letters that he knew that his efforts would not be appreciated either by strict scientists or by the church theologians. It was a very accurate prediction, still largely borne out by the treatment of his thought in professional circles. The power of Teilhard's vision is instead in its dual commitment to God *and* the world that alone can inspire the confidence, along with the trust in God and in the Spirit working through us, that this present age demands. Only by taking the *risk* of breaking through the confines of outmoded forms of thinking and formulas of belief can we hope to arrive at the renewed confidence and *security* that we so desperately crave.

Yet when all is said and done, I doubt whether on this side of eternity any so-called "universal faith" is possible as such. Perhaps the most we can expect is an all-embracing, a *"catholic"* (in the original sense of that word) openness and faithfulness to the truth wherever it is found. Just as there has always been a plurality of theological approaches within Christianity, even within the New Testament itself, we have to resign ourselves to the fact that the human race, as long as it is made up of separate peoples, with different cultures, and varying outlooks on life, will also have diverse religions, some as different as Hinduism is from Islam, or Christianity is from Buddhism. Yet each has something to contribute, because each has experienced, in its own way, something of the ultimate truth.

I may firmly believe—as I do, and as did Teilhard—that the "ever-greater Christ" will be revealed as the culmination of an on-going process by which, in humanity and through humanity, the whole cosmos is progressively united with God. Yet, even if I were to say that I knew this to be true as a result of some peak-experience of some sort or another, the habitual enjoyment of such a unitive consciousness remains provisional in this life. At best, even the highest vision of the truth remains as "a dim reflection in a mirror" (1 Cor 13:12), always on the level of the life of *faith*. Such faith demands that we always remain committed to the search for ultimate meaning—enough that we are willing to take the *risk* of recognizing it wherever and whenever it is encountered.

APPENDIX

FAITH STAGES & CRITERIA

Criteria →	A. Form of Logic	B. Form of Perspective-taking	C. Form of Moral Judgment
Stages ↙			
0/I Instinctive Faith	(Primal trust feeling)	Self-World identification	Self-gratification
1/II Intuitive Faith	Pre-operational	Rudimentary Empathy & Adaptation	Punishment & Reward
2/III Literal Faith	Concrete Operational	Simple Perspective-taking	Instrumental Hedonism
3/IV Conventional Faith	Early Formal Operations	Mutual Role-taking	Interpersonal/Law & Order
4/V Personal Faith	Formal Operational (Dichotomizing)	Interpersonal Self-selective	Reflective Relativism
5/VI Conjunctive Faith	Formal Operational (Dialectical)	Interpersonal Expanded	Universal-Critical Awareness of Higher Law
6/VII Unitive Faith	Formal Synthesizing	Universal Identification	Loyalty to Being

APPENDIX

Adapted from James W. Fowler

D. Bounds of Social Awareness	E. Locus of Authority	F. Form of World-Coherence	G. Role of Symbols
Parents &	Primary Caregivers	Trustworthy Reliability	Identical with Object
Family Circle	Parents & Parent-like Adults	Episodic & Mysterious	Magical-Numinous
Neighborhood & School	Trusted Authority Figures	Narrative-Dramatic	One-Dimensional, Literal
Community & Given Class	Class-accepted Authority Figures	Tacit System: Symbolic	Multi-Dimensional, Conventional
Chosen Class Norms & Interests	Self-chosen Authorities & Reason	Explicit System: Conceptual	Critical, Conceptual-Ideational Rejection
Critical Awareness beyond Class Norms	Collective Wisdom & Experience	Multi-Systemic	Rejoining of Symbol & Idea "Polymorphic"
Trans-class Trans-ethnic Awareness	Unified Vision vs. Ego-centrism	Unitive, Cosmic	Transparency & Complementarity

Bibliography

Babin, Pierre, *Crisis of Faith: The Religious Psychology of Adolescence* (New York: Herder & Herder, 1963). Translated by Eva Fleischner.

Baum, Gregory (ed.), *The Teachings of the Second Vatican Council* (Westminster: The Newman Press, 1966).

Bellah, Robert, *Habits of the Heart: Individualism and Commitment in American Life,* (Berkeley: University of California Press, 1985; New York: Harper & Row, 1987).

Brown, Raymond E., Fitzmyer, Joseph A., Murphy, Roland E., *The Jerome Biblical Commentary* (Englewood Cliffs: Prentice-Hall, 1968).

Catholic Biblical Association, *New Catholic Bible* (New York: Catholic Book Publishing Co., 1970).

Drummond, Richard H., *Gautama the Buddha: An Essay in Religious Understanding* (Grand Rapids: William B. Eerdmans, 1974).

Dulles, Avery, *The Survival of Dogma* (New York: Crossroad, 1982).

Dumoulin, Heinrich, S.J., *A History of Zen Buddhism* (New York: Random House, 1963; Boston: Beacon Press, 1979). Translated from the German by Paul Peachy.

Erikson, Erik H., *Young Man Luther* (New York: W.W. Norton, 1958).

——— *Gandhi's Truth* (New York: W.W. Norton, 1969).

Farley, Margaret A., *Personal Commitments: Beginning, Keeping, Changing* (New York, San Francisco: Harper & Row, 1986).

Fowler, James W., *Stages of Faith: The Psychology of Human Development and the Quest for Meaning* (New York: Harper & Row, 1981).

————— *Becoming Adult: Becoming Christian: Adult Development and Christian Faith* (New York: Harper & Row, 1984).

Frankl, Viktor E., *Man's Search for Meaning: An Introduction to Logotherapy* (New York: Pocket Books 1959, 1963).

————— *The Will to Meaning: Foundations and Applications of Logotherapy* (New York: New American Library, 1969).

————— *The Unconscious God: Psychotherapy and Theology* (New York: Simon & Schuster, 1975).

Fromm, Eric, *You Shall Be As Gods* (New York: Harcourt Brace & World, 1966).

Gallup, George, *Faith Development in the Adult Life Cycle* (module 1) (Princeton: The Gallup Organization: copyright: The Religious Education Association, 1985).

Gilligan, Carol, *In a Different Voice: Psychological Theory and Women's Development* (Cambridge: Harvard University Press, 1982).

Gorman, Margaret (ed.), *Psychology and Religion: A Reader* (New York: Paulist Press, 1985).

Helminiak, Daniel A., *Spiritual Development: An Interdisciplinary Study* (Chicago: Loyola University Press, 1987).

Huxley, Julian, *Religion Without Revelation* (New York: Mentor Books, 1957).

John of the Cross, *The Collected Works of St. John of the Cross*, translated by Kieran Kavanaugh and Otilio Rodriguez (Washington, D.C.: Institute of Carmelite Studies, 1973).

Jones, Alexander (ed.), *The Jerusalem Bible* (Garden City: Doubleday, 1966).

Jung, Carl G., *Psychological Reflections: A New Anthology of His Writings*. Selected and edited by Jolande Jacobi in collaboration with R.F.C. Hull (Bollingen Series XXXI: Princeton University Press, 1970).

Kitagawa, Joseph M., *Religions of the East* (Philadelphia: The Westminster Press, Fifth edition, 1971).

Küng, Hans, *Does God Exist? An Answer for Today* (New York: Doubleday, 1978; Random House/Vintage, 1981). Translated by Edward Quinn.

——— *Eternal Life?* (Garden City: Doubleday, 1984). Translated by Edward Quinn.

——— *Theology for the Third Millennium: An Ecumenical View* (Garden City: Doubleday, 1988). Translated by Peter Heinegg.

Leean, Constance, *Faith Development in the Adult Life Cycle* Module 2: copyright: The Religious Education Association of United States and Canada, 1985.

Loevinger, Jane, *Ego Development* (San Francisco: Jossey-Bass Publishers, 1977).

Marcel, Gabriel, *Creative Fidelity* (New York: Farrar Straus, 1964).

Maslow, Abraham H., *Religions, Values, and Peak-Experiences* (New York: Viking Books, 1970).

Merton, Thomas, *The Ascent to Truth* (New York: Harcourt, Brace & Co., 1951).

――――― *The Asian Journal of Thomas Merton* (New York: New Directions, 1973). Edited by Naomi Burton, Br. Patrick Hart & James Laughlin. Consulting Editor: Amiya Chakravarty.

Moody, Raymond A., *Life After Life* (St. Simons Id.: Mockingbird Books, 1975).

――――― *The Light Beyond* (New York: Bantam Books, 1988).

Moran, Gabriel, *Religious Education Development* (Minneapolis: Winston Press, 1983).

Mott, Michael, *The Seven Mountains of Thomas Merton* (Boston: Houghton Mifflin, 1984).

Newman, John Henry, *Essay on the Idea of the Development of Doctrine* (New York: Doubleday Image Books, 1960).

Panikkar, Raimundo, *The Trinity and the Religious Experience of Man* (New York: Orbis Books, 1973).

Rahner, Karl, *The Practice of the Faith: A Handbook of Contemporary Spirituality* (New York: Crossroad, 1984).

Rogers, Carl R., *On Becoming a Person* (Boston: Houghton Mifflin, 1961).

Smith, Wilfred Cantwell, *Faith and Belief* (Princeton: Princeton University Press, 1979).

Sweeney, Richard J., "How God Invites Us To Grow" in *Catholic Update*. Cincinnati: Franciscan Herald Press, October 1987.

Teilhard de Chardin, Pierre, *The Future of Man* (New York: Harper & Row, 1964). Translated by Norman Denny.

――― *Christianity and Evolution* (London: Collins; New York: Harper & Row, 1971). Translated by René Hague.

――― *Toward the Future* (London: Collins; New York: Harcourt Brace Jovanovich, 1975). Translated by René Hague.

Tillich, Paul, *The Dynamics of Faith* (New York: Harper & Row, 1957).

Viscott, David, *Risking* (New York: Simon & Schuster, 1977).

Watts, Alan H., *The Wisdom of Insecurity* (New York: Pantheon; Random House/Vintage, 1951).

Index